Bc

Adventure in Discipleship

Adventure in Discipleship

A Study Book by Harry C. Griffith

ZONDERVAN
PUBLISHING HOUSE

OF THE ZONDERVAN CORPORATION | GRAND RAPIDS, MICHIGAN 49506

ADVENTURE IN DISCIPLESHIP

Copyright © 1978 by Harry C. Griffith
Grand Rapids, Michigan

Library of Congress Cataloging in Publication Data

Griffith, Harry C
    Adventure in discipleship.

    Includes bibliographical references.
    1.   Christian life—1960-   I.   Title.
BV4501.2.G758   248'.4   78-23756
ISBN 0-310-37501-0

Printed in the United States of America

Contents

Introduction

In the church today, the term "discipleship" is attracting more and more attention. It is a good word and has its roots in the Bible itself. The followers of Jesus today, like those who walked with Him in Galilee, are disciples.

In our time and for many reasons the church is looking closely at what it means to "follow Jesus." Dietrich Bonhoeffer's book, *The Cost of Discipleship,* questioned the sincerity of the Christian's commitment to Jesus as his Lord and Savior. There is little doubt that Christians accept Him as Savior, but is He truly the Lord of our lives?

The answer to that question is coming from two different directions. From the Protestant tradition, through the Navigators' organization, the idea of Christians "discipling" one another has become a concept with which the church is grappling. At the same time, in the Roman Catholic Church, the Cursillo Movement arose to turn average churchgoers into Christian disciples who are changing the world.

We are coming to understand that Christian discipleship implies several things. First, it implies maturity. The disciples who lived with Jesus were led, over a period of three years, through an intensive training course which prepared them to live His message and to share it with the world. He led them toward *maturity,* toward the full development of their minds and spirits as they experienced life and coped with it through God's grace. Today, He calls His disciples to nothing less than that.

Discipleship also implies *discipline,* and discipline implies two more things. It indicates a willingness to follow a certain way, an obedience to the leader and conformity with his principles. It also suggests diligence to understand the ways of the leader and to incorporate them into one's own life.

Discipleship implies *sacrifice*. To follow another obediently and experience life reflectively, one must expect that sacrifice will be a part of the process. Bonhoeffer warned against "cheap grace." Christ called us to total commitment—full surrender—and along that way we must expect to sacrifice ourselves. The "cost of discipleship" is our ultimate gift: our very souls.

If the Christian disciple accepts his Lord's call to a disciplined, sacrificial maturity, he will want to commit his time and his very life to a search for the knowledge, enrichment, and guidance which can be found in Holy Scripture. And he will be willing to change as God molds him in the learning process.

* * *

I wish to take this opportunity to thank the Bible Reading Fellowship for the scholarship reflected in the commentaries on Scripture contained in this book, Kit Crook for her editorial help and moral support in putting it together, Lydia Dorsett who did the final editing, and my own and other Bible study groups that put this material to the test before it was published.

HARRY C. GRIFFITH

How to Use This Book

This book was designed as a study in discipleship. It can be used by one person working alone, or two people working together. It can be used for group study if the members of the group are striving earnestly for Christian maturity. The value of the study is completely dependent on the willingness of the student to examine himself honestly and to share the results of this examination with his Lord and with those with whom he studies.

There are forty chapters for forty weeks of study. Because of vacations, and other interference, it is usually assumed that twelve weeks per year are lost from the normal schedule. The book, therefore, offers a year of study for an individual or group.

The theme for each chapter is an essential element of Christian discipleship. The full year of study confronts the disciple with the vital principles of Christian maturity.

Each chapter begins with a brief introduction to a specific topic. Then a Bible passage will be read. The passage should be read prayerfully and expectantly. It should be read once to find its universal message, and read again to find the individual message the Lord may have for us.

There follows a commentary on the Scripture and its main points. Then to bring a full measure of life and experience to the passage and its principles, a story is added to illustrate its points and fix them in our memories. At the end of each chapter are four study questions for individual reflection and group discussion.

Use this study book in the way that will be most beneficial to you, or to your group.

You may study the entire session together as a group each week. Sit around a table, and be sure each participant has his own book and a pen or pencil. The leader, or teacher, may present the introduction, then guide the group in studying the week's Scripture passage. Discuss the comments and illustrations provided here. Let members of the group write out their answers to the questions, then share these answers with each other. This method will be especially helpful for new Christians who need guidance in applying Biblical principles to their daily lives. Members should review the sessions at home individually during the week.

If the members of the group wish to take more time for studying the Scripture passage in greater depth, they may study the Scripture reference at home, as well as the information provided in each chapter of this book. Then they may fill in their answers. When they meet together they may share their answers with each other. This method will be beneficial for groups who wish to spend a great deal of time in discussion. Encourage each member to share his insights, experiences, and resolutions with the others.

These studies will alert the new Christian to areas in his life where God expects growth. A person who has been a Christian for some time but who wants to experience personal growth will be able to focus special attention on areas where he feels his greatest need. Through sincere study of this book, both the new babe in Christ and the "older" Christian may take significant steps in the life-long journey toward becoming a mature Christian disciple.

1

Love and Service

The Bible, particularly the New Testament, has much to say about love. The world, also, talks about love a great deal, though often in a different sense from the Bible's interpretation of the word.

The word "love" has become so commonplace in our vocabulary that it is easy to confuse its real meaning with the meaning which the world gives it. Yet, no word—no concept—is so basic to the lives of Christians. Love is what Christ came to show us.

Therefore, as we begin to look at ourselves and at Christian discipleship, let us consider Paul's definition of love. Instead of the more familiar passage (1 Cor. 13) in which Paul writes poetically of love, let us read Romans 12:9-18. Here Paul gives us a practical, an almost "nuts and bolts," view of love.

If love is to be Christian love, it must be genuine. Paul makes clear what love is and what it is not. Verse 9 means that love must be sincere.

Every good thing has its false imitations, and love is no exception. And nothing weakens the Christian cause more severely than token good will disguised as love.

Paul, therefore, gives us some practical ways to demonstrate sincere love. First, it must have its foundation in real affection and not simply be the performance of a duty. Second, it must express itself in a genuine desire to see the best in others, "in honor, preferring (giving place to) one another." Third, it must show itself in generous giving and warm hospitality.

Rejoice together and weep together. Paul says the Christian community will be strengthened through prayer, grow in a spirit of hope and patience, and show forth love.

What demands this love places upon us! What questions it should raise in our minds concerning our own level of Christian love.

Does my concern for my fellow-man show itself to be pure by the acid tests to which Paul puts love? Do I really care for my neighbor and desire the best for him? Am I willing to show my love, not only with my lips, but in service to the ones God would have me love for Him? Is my church a fellowship of loving Christians?

The Bible makes it clear that Christ values highly the small acts of kindness which men show one another. Often, it is the most insignificant thing we do for another person that is a turning point in his life, a time when we unselfishly show God's love to one who is in more desperate need than we might know.

The Rev. Robert L. Howell, who was responsible for the Fish ministry coming to the United States, has many stories of Christian love being shown through Christian service. One of his stories he calls "Anne of the Fish."[1]

There was a Fish group in West Virginia, of the same general design of Fish groups everywhere. People could call for the miscellaneous, spur-of-the-moment help they needed and get voluntary assistance.

Anne was on duty one day and received a call from a man passing through the area who was staying in a dormitory facility provided by a local agency. The man needed diabetic medicine but did not have the money to pay for it.

Anne searched the files for someone who could help meet the man's needs, but she was unsuccessful. She let her heart overrule the policy against personal payments to solve Fish calls. She drove over to get the man, paid for his medicine, and returned him to his quarters.

Several days later there was a call for "Anne of the Fish." The man on the phone insisted that no other help from Fish would do; he wanted Anne. As there were several Annes on the Fish roster, the operator had to become a detective to locate the particular Anne the man wanted. Anne had told the man that Fish was a group of church people. He said, "I don't know what church is. I haven't been in a church in 18 years, but I would like to go with her on Sunday if she wants me." "Anne of the Fish" was not simply fulfilling a duty. She loved at a deeper level, and, as a result, one of God's children came home to church.

In what specific way or ways does the story of Anne illustrate Paul's definition of love?

_____

_____

_____

_____

What other elements of love does Paul talk about that are not fully illustrated in the story of Anne?

_____

_____

_____

_____

State how, in the coming week, you will manifest love in accordance with Paul's teaching.

_____

_____

_____

_____

Give an example of how someone showed love to you and thus influenced you to become a Christian.

_____

_____

_____

_____

2

The Light of Joy

We have reflected upon Paul's definition of love. Christian love is a fruit of the Spirit (Gal. 5:22-23) along with joy, peace, patience, kindness, goodness, fidelity, gentleness, and self-control. We shall consider the other fruits of the Spirit, beginning with joy.

The world views joy as akin to happiness. The Christian disciple knows joy has a deeper meaning. The Christian can be filled with joy at a moment of great unhappiness.

How can this be? Because joy is an inner quality dependent upon a right relationship with God. Regardless of the circumstances surrounding him, the individual is assured of God's presence within him.

A person's initial encounter with God can be a moment of great joy which overflows and is recognized by others immediately. The ongoing joy of the Christian disciple is greater, more subtle. Yet, at any moment, that joy may shine forth in its true light: the Light of Christ in the life of the disciple.

Paul had that joy amid the greatest of toils and tribulations. He had been commissioned to spread the Gospel. Let us read Second Corinthians 4:1-6 and reflect upon the joyful quality of Paul's life as he fulfilled that commission.

Paul makes it clear that he has no selfish reasons for preaching the Gospel. He has been commissioned by God to declare the truth, and that is what he is going to do in spite of the odds against him.

Some will reject the message because they are blinded by the god of this world—Satan. The supernatural powers of evil, although subordinate to God, are real. Those who follow the ways of evil find it very difficult to see the Light of Christ which Paul reveals.

Verse 6 is a reference to Genesis 1:3, "And God said, Let there be light." In the first creation, God's command brought light to the world. In re-creation through Christ, light comes to the heart of the individual. Paul had experienced his own heavenly vision of the Light of Christ on the Road to Damascus, and the Light of Christ has shone forth from the faces of His servants down through the centuries.

Father Andrew tells the story of a Portsmouth boy and his mother which gives true insight into this passage.[2]

The boy was going to sea on the following day, and his mother had spent the afternoon shopping for the simple clothes that he would take with him in the morning. He yawned during supper and was obviously tired, so his mother urged him to go to bed early that he might be prepared for the big day ahead.

As the boy went to his room he thought how he would like to get up early in the morning, make a fire, and prepare his mother a cup of tea as a last gesture of his love for her. Resolving to do so, he was soon asleep.

He awoke early, quietly slipped on his clothes, and came down the stairs in his bare feet trying to prevent any board from creaking. As he approached the kitchen, he saw a light shining under the door. When he opened it, in the light of the old paraffin lamp, he saw his mother stitching away at one of his shirts.

The lamplight fell on his mother's face. The light of the glory of God shone forth from it in such a way that all his life was affected by the realization of her love. "Mother," he cried, "have you been working at mending my clothes all night?"

"I couldn't let you go away," she said simply, "without your clothes just so." Then she told him of her love for him, and asked him to remember that every boy and girl had a mother, and to pray God that he might never do anything that would bring tears to the eyes of his mother or of anyone else's mother.

It was when he was dying that the sailor told the story. Like Paul, he could say that all his life he had been true to the heavenly vision, because he had seen a heavenly vision in the simple human face of his mother that morning in the kitchen. He saw the Light of Christ, and he could never forget it.

In what way or ways does the story of the sailor and his mother illustrate the inner quality of Christian joy?

_____

_____

_____

_____

What are the characteristics of Paul's means of spreading the Gospel as shown in the Bible passage?

_____

_____

_____

_____

What can you do in the coming week to bring the Light of Christ into the life of another?

_____

_____

_____

_____

Give an example of the Light of Christ in the life of a person you know, and discuss why you think that person was filled with joy.

_____

_____

_____

3

Consider the Lilies

Peace is another fruit of the Spirit. It should be a characteristic of the Christian disciple.

The world regards peace as freedom from hostility or strife, something you have because nothing bad is happening, or affecting you. It is the fortunate absence of something unpleasant.

Christian peace is something else altogether. It is the absence of anxiety; this peace results when we see situations and circumstances from God's point of view. The disciple can be at peace in the middle of hostility or strife.

Read Luke 12:22-34 to see how Jesus tells us to put aside anxious thoughts, that we may be filled with His peace.

Here, Jesus deals with the problem of anxiety: worry about our future needs. Anxiety can paralyze us. It can drain our energy and prevent us from making the right decisions and doing the right things.

Jesus is not encouraging His followers to be thoughtless or to fail to carry out their responsibilities to others and to themselves. Insurance, investments, and savings can be proper means of Christian stewardship. Jesus wishes to lead us away from that worry which concentrates on material things and makes them the primary focus of our attention. Anxiety reveals a basic lack of faith in God. "Your Father knoweth that you have need." He will take care of us, if we look first to Him and second to our material needs.

We are told to put our priorities in order. Our first priority should be the Kingdom of God. As our first concern, we should bring ourselves and everyone else into a personal relationship with Jesus Christ that He may be Lord of our lives. If that is truly our goal, our hearts will be fixed on Him.

If we are ready and willing to do the will of God, we can be sure that He will make us able by providing for our material needs. We must realize, however, that God's estimate of our requirements may be much less than our own.

Larry Christenson, a Lutheran pastor, tells a story about a young housewife who came to him for advice about her future needs.[3] She was thinking of going to work despite the fact that she had two small children at home. Her husband needed some additional education, and getting this education would reduce their income for a while.

The housewife didn't see how her family could make ends meet unless she went to work. Christenson concluded, after the discussion, that the children needed their mother more than they needed what the additional income would buy. He said, "You'd better get used to beans for a while, and stay at home."

That evening when the husband came home, he said that he had come to the same conclusion. It just wasn't the thing to do for the wife to go to work; they would simply have to manage things some other way.

The couple agreed that God's will had been revealed to them, "even though they hated beans." They stopped worrying. The anxiety left them.

Several days later a young widow came to see Pastor Christenson about a problem she had: finding someone who could take care of her little boy during the day while she worked. She had been using a variety of babysitters, which was upsetting to the child. Christenson remembered the other young woman. Perhaps there was a solution to both problems.

The young widow and the housewife got together and worked out an arrangement for the housewife to take care of the widow's child. She could stay at home with her children, and the amount the widow could pay for the babysitting was exactly the amount she had felt she needed to supplement her husband's income.

The mutual problems had been placed in God's hands, through the working of His Church, and God had once again provided for His children. Our Father knows what we need.

In what practical way or ways does Pastor Christenson's story illustrate how a disciple can be at peace?

_____

_____

_____

_____

What do you think are the major points in Jesus' teaching concerning anxiety?

_____

_____

_____

_____

Think of something you have been worrying about and state how—now or within the coming week—you are going to deal with that anxiety.

_____

_____

_____

_____

Give an example of a critical time in your life when you were filled with peace which was obviously a gift from God. Or, tell about a situation in which you would feel the need for God's peace.

_____

_____

_____

_____

4

The Patience of Job

Another fruit of the Spirit is patience. I never think of patience without recalling the remark, "Never pray for patience unless you're prepared to receive what God might send to teach you patience!"

Patience is truly hard for us to attain, particularly in the activist, instant-everything world in which we live. The shape of our whole society is mounted to do battle against waiting. The only thing the world seems willing to wait for is death.

It is easy to believe, then, that patience comes as a result of God's grace. It must be the work of the Spirit within us, because it is so foreign to our human nature.

Read James 5:7-11 for a biblical viewpoint on patience.

The early church looked to the Second Coming of the Lord as only a brief time away. James urged his brethren to be patient until then. He used a homespun illustration to make his point: the farmer can do nothing to speed the maturing of his crop; he must wait patiently for the rains.

James knew the problems that the church was encountering. As it grew, as it lived in community, as it faced a hostile world, tempers flared and voices grumbled. These people lived in the freshness of a new Kingdom rung in by Jesus' death and resurrection so few years before. They saw the possibility of perfection, but their humanity hung on them like a pall.

While they waited, they must grow in faith. They must not blame one another for the problems which surrounded them. James cautioned them not to break the commandment which forbade them to judge one another (Matt. 7:1). He warned them that judgment by Him who is fit to judge would be the consequence.

Having warned them, James then gave good examples for Christians to follow. The prophets were particularly long-suffering. They endured patiently.

There was Job, the example that even non-Christians and non-Jews use to explain patience. But Job was patient in a very active way. The story of his life shows concern about his plight, questioning of the arguments of his "friends," and a search for God. The patience of Job is exemplified in the fact that, despite it all, he never lost faith in God.

Our memories are undoubtedly sprinkled with saints who have endured the "slings and arrows of outrageous fortune." I have a mental picture of Monica praying patiently that her brilliant but wayward son Augustine would one day find the Lord. When he did, he became one of the most powerful Christian figures the world has known, the "victim" of a mother's long-suffering love.

I can also think of a saint I am privileged to know who labors patiently in the vineyard of the Lord each day. The story he shared with me reflects the kind of patience of which the Epistle of James speaks.

George (as I will call my friend) has a passion to share Christ with others. He is a true evangelist and has led many people into a living relationship with our living Lord. Yet George never pushes a person into a precipitous decision.

When George's sister discovered she was dying of cancer and moved south to be nearer George, the temptation to push her into the arms of the Lord was great, but he resisted. He was willing to have faith in God's timing. George simply remained open, prayed, and waited.

After months, the first breakthrough came—an interest in having a Bible. It was, however, only a small crack in the door and was followed by longer months of no response to the Bible, no questions, no pleas for help. George waited and prayed as his sister dropped to 80 pounds in weight and began to lose round after round in her battle to live.

Then, finally, the door opened. "George, do you believe in reincarnation?" the sister asked.

"No," replied George, "as a Christian I do not." There was then an agonizingly long pause before the next question came, but it did.

"George, what do you believe?" By the time that question had been answered adequately, the sister prayed to receive Christ as her Lord and Savior. As she slips through the last few days before she meets Him face to face, her life radiates the anticipation of that divine encounter.

The spiritual fruit known as patience had served George well. It had revealed itself in him in perhaps its purest form: patience is a willingness to live according to God's time-table despite our natural, human desire to move at our own pace.

Why was patience of critical importance in the story of George and his sister?

_____

_____

_____

_____

Job demonstrates "active" patience, George "passive" patience. The prophets often endured torment; Monica prayed. List several different characteristics, or manifestations, of patience and think of an example of each.

_____

_____

_____

_____

16 • *Adventure In Discipleship*

What can you do in the coming week to allow God to manifest the fruit of patience in your life?

_____

_____

_____

What was the "most patient" thing you ever did or endured? How did you feel about it?

_____

_____

_____

_____

5

Making Our Faith Personal

Another fruit of the Spirit is kindness. In the past, I have had a rather limited view of kindness—patting a child on the head, for instance, or opening a door for a little old lady with a heavy package.

From a Christian point of view, kindness is much more involved than such acts of superficial goodness. *The New Bible Commentary: Revised* defines what Paul meant by kindness in Galatians 5:22:

Kindness denotes excellence of character in the sense of a due regard for the fragile nature of human personality and for human need.[4]

Kindness carries with it a keen sensitivity to the needs of others, and a desire to meet those needs.

In Luke 19:1-10, we get a good picture of how Jesus put kindness into practice.

Jesus reached out to Zaccheus. Perhaps He had known Zaccheus before the incident mentioned in the Bible passage; there is no way for us to know. Jesus' sensitivity was so great that He could understand what it meant for a small, wealthy man, chief of the publicans, to climb up a sycamore tree in order to see Him pass by.

In any event, it was Jesus who spoke. He called Zaccheus by name and invited Himself to Zaccheus' house. By climbing that tree, Zaccheus had gone as far as he could to humble himself. Jesus acknowledged that act and brought it to fulfillment. All that was necessary to bring Zaccheus to the point of repentance and the beginning of a new life was the openness and acceptance of our Lord.

Jesus gave Zaccheus the gift of friendship. He passed through

Jericho on the way to Jerusalem and the Cross, and He would not pass that way again.

Being sensitive to others is essential for effective Christian ministry. It is of primary importance to live a life of openness to the needs and feelings, thoughts and aspirations of those around us. We should be able to respond to the unspoken request, to see below the surface of events, to sense the feelings behind the things that are said. We desperately need to listen, with our ears and all of the sensitivity God gives us, and to bring to reality what the other person does not have the ability to ask or pray for.

Jesus did that for Zaccheus and completely turned his life around.

Keith Miller tells what happened to him when he saw the need to express his faith in the personal relationships that were laid before him day by day.[5] On the way to work one day, he stopped at the service station he had been patronizing for several years. When the station attendant said, "Good morning, Mr. Miller," he was shocked to realize that he had seen that man many times and yet had never really noticed him as a person and had no idea what his name was.

Glancing at the man's name tag, Keith Miller said, "Good morning, Charlie," and sought to start a conversation with the man. He felt that he had ignored the man for years, but now was interested in him as a person. "Say, Charlie, do you have a family?"

That started a conversation that led to a first-name friendship. The service station attendant had a large family, and later, when one of the man's children was seriously injured in an accident, Keith Miller was able to respond as a concerned friend rather than as a "Christmas basket Christian."

Every day we each face a multitude of opportunities to be sensitive to the people around us, to let them know that we care about them individually. Jesus gave us a good example in His contact with Zaccheus. It is up to us to follow His example.

To what risks, inconveniences, and other possible problems did Keith Miller open himself by starting a real conversation with Charlie?

_____

_____

_____

In what ways did Jesus demonstrate kindness to Zaccheus?

_____

_____

_____

_____

In what ways could you demonstrate kindness to a Charlie or a Zaccheus in the coming week?

_____

_____

_____

_____

Think of a situation in which you did or did not exercise Christian kindness. If you did not, what could you have done differently?

_____

_____

_____

_____

6

Choosing Sides

At this point it may be helpful to pause in our study of the fruit of the Spirit and look at some other basics of discipleship. We will return to the other fruit later in the book.

Let us consider the seriousness of our call to be Christ's disciples and the sincerity with which we accept that call. I remember the time I was "hit in the face" with C. S. Lewis' statement that we have a choice of the way we regard Jesus Christ.

> I am trying here to prevent anyone saying the really foolish thing that people often say about Him: 'I'm ready to accept Jesus as a great moral teacher, but I don't accept His claim to be God.' That is the one thing we must not say. A man who was merely a man and said the sort of things Jesus said would not be a great moral teacher. He would either be a lunatic or else he would be the Devil of Hell. You must make your choice. Either this man was, and is, the Son of God; or else a madman or something worse. You can shut Him up for a fool, you can spit at Him and kill Him as a demon; or you can fall at His feet and call Him Lord and God. But let us not come with any patronising nonsense about His being a great human teacher. He has not left that open to us. He did not intend to.[6]

Now read Matthew 12:22-37 to see how Jesus Himself dealt with this question.

The Spirit of God was upon Jesus, and He was able to cast devils out of those who were possessed, as well as to perform various healing miracles. Jesus brought to the world a new age in which God's Holy Spirit showed forth in power. That is why John the Baptist told of the coming baptism of the Spirit. Jesus demonstrated the power of the Spirit through the working of miracles.

The Pharisees once again attacked Jesus, this time by arguing that the Spirit of God through which Jesus acted was in fact Beelzebub, the prince of devils. In so doing, the Pharisees blasphemed against the Holy Spirit. God will forgive those who do not recognize Jesus as the Son of God if they eventually come to him. But those who see the miracles and say they are the work of Satan will not be forgiven. The Pharisees denied in Jesus what they recognized in their own case: that the power to cast out devils comes from God.

In a parable, Jesus pointed out that Satan was being bound and was powerless. That Jesus could cast out devils while Satan was helpless shows that God is active in the world and has the power to overcome Satan. (The "strong man" in the parable is Satan, and "his goods" are those possessed by devils; Satan's "house" being robbed demonstrates that the end of his age had come upon the world through Jesus.)

Words are more than sounds. They are an outward reflection of inward attitudes. They are evidence of attitudes of life just as the quality of fruit is evidence of the quality of the tree upon which it grows. Therefore, in judging the world, God will judge men according to the words which reflect the attitude of their hearts. What men say surely indicates what they are.

Jesus is laying His position on the line. Those who hear Him must choose; they are either for Him or they are against Him.

C. S. Lewis wrote a little parable of his own on this matter of choosing sides.[7] He noted that when the author walks onto the stage at the end of a play, the play is over. When we face God, He will have "walked upon the stage" of life. What good will it do us then to say that we have been on His side?

We will see the natural world fading away like a dream, and coming suddenly upon us will be beauty that our limited minds could never imagine. Yet, what is perfect beauty to us may be ghastly to others. What choice is left? Then we will face God as He is. That is a fact so overwhelming that every creature will be filled with either irresistible love or irresistible horror. At that time, the opportunity for choosing sides will have passed. Then we will discover which side we truly have chosen.

How do you honestly feel about the time when you will meet God face to face, whether through death or at the Second Coming?

_____

_____

_____

_____

What does the Bible passage tell us about our attitudes, and how we reflect our faith by what we say and do?

_____

_____

_____

_____

What may impede your being as bold a witness as Christ would have you be, and what are you going to do so that people will know which side you have chosen?

_____

_____

_____

_____

Relate a situation in which it was necessary for you to confront someone about his/her need to "choose sides"; what were the results?

_____

_____

_____

_____

7

The Peanut Prayer

Prayer is as essential as any ingredient in the life of the Christian disciple. It is his lifeline to God. Yet, I have never met the person who was completely happy with his prayer life.

Few things are as multi-faceted as prayer. As I write this, I will soon be participating in the sixth annual prayer dialogue of a group of approximately twenty-five church leaders from eight Christian denominations. Each year for a full weekend we have discussed our own prayer lives, and we have never had a dull moment.

There is no doubt that God wants us to pray. The question is how we may pray most effectively.

Read Matthew 7:7-11 to see what Jesus says about prayer.

When you pray, make sure you are seeking the right thing. So taught Dr. E. Stanley Jones, the great evangelist. Using this passage as his text, he told his students, "Whatever you really set your heart upon, you will achieve, whether it be wealth, or power, or pleasure, none of which in itself satisfies. Make sure you are seeking the right things."

We may ask, does God really answer our prayers? Yes, He always does, though not always in the exact way in which we ask. Earlier, I mentioned Monica, the mother of St. Augustine, who prayed for years for her son's conversion. When she learned that he was leaving for Rome, she prayed that God would stop him from leaving her. Augustine left, but he was converted.

In a familiar Bible story, the mother of James and John begged Jesus to grant her sons positions of honor on either side of Him in the Kingdom. Jesus did not grant her request; but James was one of the first persons to die for His Lord, and John remained a beloved leader of the church. God indeed honored them in due time.

On the other hand, the penitent thief who was crucified with Jesus received immediately all that he asked.

Is there a pattern? We can be sure that God answers our prayers because Jesus has promised that He does. God never gives a stone to him who asks for bread. The key is to ask for bread, to seek that which God would have us pray for in accordance with His will.

Larry Christenson tells an interesting story about the famous scientist George Washington Carver.[8] Carver, a great man of prayer, went out into the woods one morning to pray for wisdom.

Dr. Carver said, "Lord, why did you make the world?"

The reply was, "Little man, that's too big for you. Ask something smaller."

Then Carver said, "Lord, why did you make man?"

And, again, the answer came back, "Little man, that's still too big for you. Ask for something smaller."

Dr. Carver thought for some time, and then he asked, "Lord, why did you make the peanut?"

"That's just your size," came the reply. And Carver went, as a man of prayer and a man of God, into his laboratory and discovered 153 uses for the peanut.

Do you believe that the story of Dr. Carver is simply an example of his humility, or do you believe that God speaks to His disciples in that manner?

_____

_____

_____

_____

What do you know about prayer from Jesus' teaching in the passage from Matthew?

_____

_____

_____

_____

What are the weak areas in your prayer life, and how will you improve them in the coming week?

_____

_____

_____

_____

What is the most dramatic example of answered prayer you have experienced?

_____

_____

_____

_____

8

Blessed Are the Feet

The Christian disciple has been commissioned by the Lord to carry the Gospel to the ends of the earth, and across the street.

Some people are specifically called to work in the mission field, at home or abroad. Others are given the gift of evangelism by God and have a burning desire to lead others to a commitment to Christ as Lord and Savior of their lives. All of us should know how to tell others what the Lord has done in our lives, who Jesus Christ is and what He did for all mankind, and how to pray with another to receive Christ.

We should be sowing seeds of God's love in all that we do, that people may be led to the Lord. God works with us, through us, and in us in a multitude of ways His purposes to fulfill, if we are open to His leading.

Paul had a particular gift of evangelism. Read Romans 10:11-21.

In this passage, Paul makes it clear that the way to God is through faith and trust (as opposed to the way of works and of legalism), and that it is a way open to all men. It is not a new doctrine that God's salvation is available for all races of mankind. Step by step, Paul showed that the message has been given.

First, quoting from Isaiah, he demonstrates that the message had been given to the Jews. Then using Deuteronomy 32:21 and Isaiah 65:1 as his authority, he shows that God's salvation is offered even to the Gentiles. He is saying that there is no excuse for ignorance of God's message.

Although Paul seems to be arguing with those to whom he is

writing, he is trying to tell them about the joy of sharing the Good News of God's love and forgiveness. The Jews may have been too bound by their own prejudices to accept the message. If so, their failure robs them of the joy which that message conveys; it does not limit God.

Paul is so filled with the joy of proclaiming Jesus Christ that he is heartbroken over those who, for one reason or another, cannot hear the message. There are many people who can know better, if they really want to, as Paul makes clear in this passage.

There are many more, however, who do not know, and "how beautiful are the feet of them that preach the gospel of peace, and bring glad tidings of good things!" The joy of carrying that Good News is not limited to a few carefully chosen people. The "gospel of peace" is to be spread by each Christian, and God gives us opportunities to do so in ways that are natural to us.

God gets His message across when Christians are willing to be the instruments of His "gospel of peace." Father Andrew tells the story of the Lorraines, a missionary couple who took Christianity to the Lakher tribe in Ossam.[9] This mountain tribe of headhunters had heard about Christianity from a neighboring tribe, and the Lorraines answered the call to teach this new religion to the Lakhers.

Lorraine did his best to show the love of God by caring for the sick and in many other ways. Wherever he went, he took pencil and paper with him, trying to learn the language of the tribe. However, it was impossible for him to learn the language sufficiently to write even one verse of Scripture in the Lakher's native tongue.

Then God did something very beautiful. A baby girl was born to the Lorraines. The tribal people hailed the little white wonder as a princess in their midst. By growing up with the Lakher children, the little girl learned their language quite naturally and taught it to her father. Thus, a small child was able to lead a tribe of headhunters to the knowledge of the love of Christ, that they might be taught "the gospel of peace."

What does the story of the Lorraines tell us about God's faithfulness in meeting the needs of those who are obedient to Him?

_____

_____

_____

_____

What points are made by Paul in the Scripture passage?

_____

_____

_____

_____

Are you willing to pray to share Christ with another person during the coming week? Why or why not?

_____

_____

_____

_____

Give an example from your personal experience or observation of how God works "in mysterious ways" to lead people to Himself.

_____

_____

_____

_____

9

It Is I

The Christian disciple must have a dual companionship: the friendship of his Lord and the loyalty and support of his brothers and sisters in Christ.

In answer to people who thought they could be Christians "on their own," Sam Shoemaker used the illustration of two logs burning brightly in a fire. When the logs were separated, the fire in each log quickly burned out. The warmth of human love is an important ingredient in our life of faith.

It is the nature of faith itself that it go on amid doubt and turmoil. In the spiritual valleys through which we all must pass, we seek not only our Lord but also our Christian brothers and sisters.

In our Bible passage, John 6:15-24, Jesus was both Lord and Friend.

Jesus went away to be alone and His disciples boarded a boat to cross the Sea of Galilee. They were to meet later on the other side. While He was praying, Jesus undoubtedly perceived that the disciples were caught in a storm at sea, and He went to be with them.

When the disciples saw Jesus, they were afraid. We can imagine their reaction when, struggling against the sea, they looked up and saw the figure of their Master coming toward them! "Be not afraid," He says. "It is I."

Both as the church and as individual Christians we need the presence of Jesus. Whatever our need, He comes to us, encourages us, enlightens and strengthens us, and brings us to our goals. When we "take Him in" as the disciples took Him into the boat, He changes our lives to what they are supposed to be. The New Testament is filled with stories of men and women whose lives were completely turned around because they took Jesus in. They can be our examples.

Paul is a particularly good example. Here was a man who threw into prison those who followed Jesus. Then he, too, met Jesus on the road to Damascus. He "took Jesus in" and allowed Jesus to take over his life. What a turnabout he made!

In our Bible passage, the crowds were baffled by what had happened to Jesus. He had gotten away from them. Apparently He was not with His disciples, so they went seeking Him. They may have sought Him for the wrong reasons, but they went after Him nonetheless.

Many people seek Jesus today and for many reasons. They need the assurance that He is with them and cares for them. Very often it is through us to others that Jesus conveys the message, "It is I."

Father Andrew tells a story of two men who were close friends in the First World War.[10] During a battle, one man found that the other had been wounded and lay in "no man's land" beyond the protection of the trench. He begged the officer in charge to allow him to go to his wounded friend and bring him back to the trench.

At first the officer refused because the area where the injured man lay was raked continually with gunfire. Finally, however, he gave in simply because the man pleaded so earnestly to go after his comrade.

The man crept out through the gunfire to where his friend lay and brought him back to the trench where the officer was standing. The friend was dead and the man was mortally wounded. "My poor fellow," said the officer, "I told you there was no point in your going. You see it was not worthwhile. Your pal is dead, and you are wounded."

"Oh, but it was well worthwhile," replied the man. "Before he died, my friend said, 'I knew you would come.'" There were two men in the midst of vicious combat who had peace in their own souls.

We may be in the worst of surroundings or situations and have peace within our souls. In all such places and times, Jesus is always there to those who are ready to receive Him. To them He says, "It is I; be not afraid."

Why was it worthwhile for the soldier to give his life even though he could not save his friend's life?

_____

_____

_____

_____

What elements in the Bible passage show Jesus' divinity? What shows Him as a true friend?

_____

_____

_____

_____

Is there someone to whom you should go and say, in Christ's name, "It is I"?

_____

_____

Think of an instance in which a Christian friend showed (or failed to show) to you the loyalty and support of the soldier in the story. How did you respond?

_____

_____

_____

10

In God's Time

A Christian learns many things as he grows in discipleship. One of the most important things he learns is the ability to distinguish between the Lord's guidance and the challenge of the world.

We learn to recognize the still, small voice of the Lord (when He chooses to communicate with us in that manner) after we have walked closely with Him day by day. We come into an intimate relationship with the Good Shepherd through worship, prayer, Bible study, and by bringing people into contact with the Christian life. The closer we are to Him, the more clearly we understand His subtle guidance. The more obediently we follow Him, the easier it is to hear and understand Him.

The reverse, of course, is true. If, because of our own selfish desires, we are insensitive to the Lord's guidance, it becomes more and more difficult to hear His voice.

John 10:11-26 illustrates the point.

Jesus' description of Himself as the Good Shepherd is of critical importance. Unlike the hired hand who flees in time of danger, Jesus is the Shepherd who is prepared to die to protect His flock. In doing so, He accomplishes the will of His Father. To those with "ears to hear," Jesus clearly reveals His role as the Messiah.

Moreover, Jesus distinguishes between the folds of sheep who know His voice. In verse 16, "this fold" refers to the Jewish nation; then Jesus mentions "other sheep," who are the Gentiles. Jesus envisions those of His own who will come from the Gentiles as well as from the Jewish people. It is not being a part of the flock that is important; it is hearing and following the Shepherd.

The Jewish leaders did not accept such claims on Jesus' part; they failed to hear "His voice." They wanted "signs and wonders" which, as Jesus pointed out, they would still refuse to believe. Their sentence is given by Jesus: "Ye are not of my sheep."

As sheep of the Good Shepherd, Christians can hear Jesus' voice. Rosalind Rinker tells how she distinguished the voice of the Good Shepherd in a situation she faced in China years ago.[11]

She had recently moved into a small apartment, and while she was studying Chinese in one room, a carpenter was working on a cupboard in the other room. Miss Rinker began to get "nudgings" to talk to the carpenter and tell him about Christ.

"Aren't you going to talk to the carpenter? You'd better do something. How long are you going to wait? He's there." These thoughts kept running around in her head. She felt real pressure to do something.

Then she thought of what Jesus had said, "My sheep know My voice and they follow Me," and she recognized immediately that the voice she had been hearing was not the Shepherd's voice.

With relief, Miss Rinker prayed, "Lord, I don't believe it was You who spoke. You never push, and you're never in a hurry. You know I'm ready to do everything You want me to do. Please give me the patience of a quiet heart that I may hear You when You are ready to speak."

With that assurance, Miss Rinker settled down to her work. Later, in a perfectly natural way which resulted from the carpenter's question about a Christian poster-picture in the room, she was able to talk to him about Jesus Christ and to teach him to pray.

Miss Rinker had learned to recognize the still, quiet voice of the Good Shepherd. She was prepared to obey that voice and not the voice of this world which would deceive us, frustrate us, and lead us astray.

Should we not be ready at all times to witness for the Lord? Why should not Rosalind Rinker have jumped at the first opportunity to talk about Christ to the Chinese carpenter?

_____

_____

_____

_____

In this Gospel passage, what does Jesus teach us about Himself which can help us understand Him and better hear His voice?

_____

_____

_____

_____

In what ways do you feel that you have not listened to the Lord's voice?

_____

_____

_____

_____

Think of an instance in your own life when you were tempted to follow a false voice, waited, and then heard the voice of the Good Shepherd. What happened?

_____

_____

_____

11

Hope in Sacrifice

Christian disciples occupy paradoxical roles. On the one hand, they are the adopted sons of the King, the brothers and sisters of Jesus Himself. On the other hand, they are servants to the world.

We don't hear enough these days about the servanthood to which we as Christians are called. Suffering for the sake of others may be discussed in theory, but we see precious little of it in practice. Yet, we are not fulfilling our calling until we are ready to lay down our lives for others.

Why should Christians be willing to sacrifice and suffer for others? Because their hope is not in the rewards of the world. We are inheritors of a greater Kingdom, and we live in the vibrant hope of that life to come.

Paul talks about this hope in Romans 8:18-30.

This is a passage about hope. All of life is a call toward something we do not yet see. We know that a new life is possible for us, not only here on earth, but also on the other side of the eternal life which Christians possess. The center of that possibility, the reason for that hope, is Jesus.

We do not see Jesus as He is. We need only look at history and at our own past lives to know that man has never measured up to Jesus. Yet, we have hope.

We know the evil that we face in the world. We know the sufferings we can expect. We know the frustration that lies ahead of us as we (amidst our own weakness and the many temptations of the world) try to live as Jesus would have us live. These things are not yet eliminated, but they give us the opportunity to endure because we have hope.

Through Christ, fear and suffering and frustration are being transformed, changed in such a manner that they have no victory over us. As we grow in our understanding of Jesus, who He is and what He has done for us, our fears fall into the background, our pain is not so great, and our frustrations do not control our lives.

It is Jesus within us who gives us hope. His Spirit prays within us even when we do not know what we should pray. God knows each of us personally and calls us according to His purposes, so that the things of our life work together for good. As we sacrifice ourselves in obedience to God, His purposes are fulfilled in us. We see only glimpses of His glory now compared to what we will understand and experience when we are fully in the presence of God.

Hope in the midst of suffering was well described by Ernest Gordon.[12] Complete demoralization existed in the Japanese prison camps along the Kwai River during World War II. Allied prisoners by the thousands died of exhaustion, malnutrition, and disease. Men were viciously tortured. They gave up hope and turned into depraved creatures, even stealing food from their dying comrades.

Then a miracle occurred. A handful of Christians began to change the condition in the prison camps. They gave away what food they had to those in greater need. They forsook sleep to minister to the sick and the dying.

Suddenly a glimmer of hope shone through as the Spirit of Christ touched those beaten men. They discovered the joy of serving others where there was no other joy.

Sacrifice bore the fruit of hope.

Some portions of Scripture were copied painfully by hand, and a Bible study began. Worship services were held to meet the men's increasing interest in God and what He was doing in their lives. Men were healed and lives were transformed by God's grace. A sense of direction and a feeling of worth filled the camps. The sacrifice of a few, in obedience to God's call, brought hope in a hopeless situation.

Why were the men who were already starving willing to eat less in order to share their food with others?

_____

_____

_____

_____

List the reasons for hope Paul mentions in the passage from Romans.

_____

_____

_____

_____

What sacrifice is God asking you to make on behalf of someone else?

_____

_____

_____

_____

Think of some instance in which you suffered for another person, or another suffered for you, as an act of Christian love. How did you feel about it?

_____

_____

_____

_____

_____

12

The Busy Man

Sacrifice is a relative thing. It can involve real suffering, like the suffering considered in our last chapter. Or it can be the simple pain of obedience, giving up something we want, yielding to an inconvenience. The key to the meaning of our actions is what those actions reveal of our heart. Our heart and our "treasure" are likely to be in the same place.

What will we not give up for the sake of our Lord? That is not a question we deal with one time and then forget. We face it every day; there is always something more we have not yielded. We're thankful that every time we give up some of our own private territory for the Lord's sake, we grow in His grace. He always gives us more than we give Him, though what He gives may be of a different nature than what we yield.

Unfortunately, not everyone yields. Read Luke 18:18-30.

The story of the rich young ruler is one of the saddest in the Bible. He was a man with much potential who obviously had been touched by what he saw in Jesus. He wanted what Jesus had to give—eternal life—but, in the end, he was not willing to pay the price.

The fact that the man had great wealth was not the only problem. Jesus did not tell every rich man He encountered to sell his possessions. Nicodemus and Joseph of Arimathea were wealthy, but we have no evidence that Jesus required them to do as He commanded the rich young ruler.

The fact was that this young man's wealth was standing in the way of his faith. For him it was a burden he could not afford to carry. God deals with each of us in His own way according to our special needs and problems. The command He gives one person may be very different from what He tells another. "Follow me" applies to us all, but "sell all that thou hast" was a special command to the rich young ruler.

The man who pursues wealth and God at the same time has a difficult task. God alone can save him from the danger of being possessed by his possessions. The pursuit of wealth tends to focus a person's attention solely on the world and what it has to offer. Also, as a person gains financial independence he is inclined to develop a sense of self-sufficiency; he forgets his dependence on God.

The humility to receive what God has to give seldom goes hand in hand with the acquisition of great wealth. Those who were with Jesus asked, "Who then can be saved?" for they thought that a rich man had the best chance of salvation. He was the one with time to observe the details of the Law, with money to give alms. How little they understood the ways of God.

We see another interesting reaction. Peter wanted to be sure that Jesus realized what the disciples had given up to follow Him. However, it is a mistake to think highly of ourselves for our sacrifices for Christ's sake. It is sufficient that we are given opportunities to serve in His Kingdom and to live eternally with Him.

Many business executives today suffer from the same problems that beset the rich young ruler. Keith Miller tells about a busy man who came to understand that the world and its ways, and not Jesus, were running his life.[13]

One morning as he was rushing to catch a train to work, he made a decision to let Christ rule his life for that day. In spite of his pressing schedule, he resolved to be a Christian in the personal contacts he would experience. Jesus (rather than speaking engagements and administrative duties) would reign in his heart.

By the time the executive had picked up his train ticket, he was running late. Hurrying across the lobby with his briefcase and his other paraphernalia, he heard the last "all aboard." He reached the train just in time, but as he attempted to step aboard he bumped into a small boy carrying a jigsaw puzzle. The puzzle fell to the platform and scattered in every direction.

The busy man stopped and looked down at the tears in the child's eyes. With an inward sigh, he smiled and (as the train pulled out) stooped down to help the boy pick up his puzzle. In fascination, the child watched the man pick up all of the pieces. "Mister," he asked, "are you Jesus?"

The man realized that, for that moment on that platform, he had been.

Why did the boy think the businessman was Jesus, and what does this tell us about a child's concept of Jesus?

_____

_____

_____

_____

What principles in Jesus' teaching in the Gospel passage do we need to note for our future guidance?

_____

_____

_____

_____

What is "possessing you" that you need to yield to the Lord?

_____

_____

_____

_____

Consider a time when the Lord confronted you with something you had not yielded to Him. What did you do, and what were the results?

_____

_____

_____

_____

13

Confrontation

In previous chapters, we have considered the ways the Lord speaks to us and the various ways we yield ourselves to Him.

Rosalind Rinker listened for the gentle voice of the Good Shepherd and responded to it. Men in war, because of the hope that was in them, suffered for their brothers. We have seen how God asks us to give up those things which separate us from Him. Inner conviction is the common element in all these instances.

Sometimes the Lord speaks to us "loud and clear." He confronts us in no uncertain terms because our condition, our attitudes, and perhaps our prejudices make it almost impossible for us to hear Him.

He spoke this way to Peter in Acts 10:1-48.

Peter had been conditioned by his background and prejudices to regard the Gentiles as unclean. It was easy for him to understand the command to preach to the Gentiles, but it was difficult for him to treat them as equals. A confrontation was necessary if God's purpose was to be fulfilled.

God is ever working to bring His plans to fruition. Cornelius longed to come into closer relationship with the Lord, and through God's intervention he was prompted to send to Peter for help.

At the same time, through a vision, God was preparing Peter. Peter was confronted with what he understood to be unclean, yet God told him to kill and eat. Peter refused to eat what to him was unclean and common. The Lord spoke to him again, "What God hath cleansed, call not thou unclean."

Peter had come to understand half of the picture when the messengers from Cornelius arrived to request that he return with them to Caesarea. Peter had already realized the significance of his rooftop vision, and when he heard what God had said to Cornelius all the pieces fell together. Cornelius and his family were baptized and welcomed into the greater family of the Lord.

Peter might well have missed a gentle, quiet nudge from the Lord. Confrontation and confirmation were what he needed, and he got both.

A number of years ago the Lord confronted me in a similar manner. As I had grown more and more aware of Him and His work in my life, I had turned over to Him bits and pieces of myself. I was, however, in a responsible position with a large corporation, and I had not been able to reconcile all of my work with my faith.

Although I prayed through the various crises of my work, I did not expect much to result from my prayer. I grew anxious because of my lack of authority to effect changes in the company. I had prayed casually about the matter, but finally I became desperate.

"You have to help me, Lord!" I pleaded.

To my dismay, the reply came back "loud and clear," "Stop drinking."

I couldn't believe it. What I had been praying about had nothing to do with my drinking alcoholic beverages, and I did not drink to excess. I reminded the Lord that some of my best Christian witnessing had been given at cocktail parties. Yet, in the awesomeness of that confrontation, God was not to be denied.

I compromised. "Lord," I said, "I'll give up drinking for pleasure, but I can't believe that You want me to give up alcohol forever."

A month later things were no better, and I prayed again in desperation. I got the same answer. (I had asked for a small exception for wine and beer, but that, too, was denied.) I yielded.

Immediately, beautiful things began to happen to me. I was promoted in the company and was given the authority to make the changes for which I had prayed. More significant than that, however, was the beginning of a series of events which, a year later, led me into fulltime Christian work.

In the midst of my routine work and my routine prayers I never would have heard a still, small voice telling me to stop drinking. It was necessary for me to be confronted, and it changed my life.

Every now and then I would like to have a drink, but I can't, for I am reminded of the relationship I have with the God who created the universe.

What similarities and what differences are there in Peter's confrontation and in mine?

_____

_____

_____

_____

What was the eternal significance of God's confrontation with Peter?

_____

_____

_____

_____

As a result of this study, have you been confronted by God? In what way?

_____

_____

_____

_____

Tell of an instance when God has confronted you.

_____

_____

_____

14

In the Name of Jesus

The Christian disciple exercises the authority he has been given by the Lord he serves. There is power in the name of Jesus to combat Satan and to bring healing and reconciliation to the world. We are ambassadors, emissaries of the King. We are Christ in the world today—His feet, His arms, His voice.

As good ambassadors, we should understand this authority and function within its bounds. We should understand the diversity of situations we may face; we should be aware of the variety of gifts we have to bring God's healing grace into those situations.

We often use intercessory prayer as a last resort, when it should come first. If our child is ill, we should get medical help. But the first thing we should do is to pray for healing.

Read Acts 3:1-10 to see what healing was wrought through Peter and John.

During His ministry, Jesus healed people and performed a variety of miraculous acts. He spoke with authority, and things happened. Furthermore, He told His followers that they would do greater works than His (John 14:12).

Peter and John healed a crippled man "in the name of Jesus Christ of Nazareth." "Name" here represents the authority of Jesus' disciples to continue the wondrous works which He had begun.

Jesus had proclaimed the Kingdom of God, God's authority over human life. In Him the Kingdom had become flesh. The apostles shared in the authority of Jesus (Luke 9:1) during His time on earth, and their work in Acts was a continuation of that which began in the name of Jesus before His ascension.

In a sense, Chapter 29 of Acts is being written now. Today we are called to speak and act in the name of Jesus so that the world may be healed. Only as the church lives in the name of Jesus will it have the authority to be what it is called to be.

That the church has something more powerful than money is illustrated by Cecil B. Murphey.[14] He tells about Jenny, who, after completing two years of college, was to spend the summer doing missionary work in the Dominican Republic. The local church leaders felt they could give Jenny only a small honorarium to help her in her work. They, like Peter and John, had to say, "Silver and gold have I none, but such as I have give I thee." What they had to give was their love and concern for Jenny and daily support of her in their prayers.

Not being content with general prayers for Jenny's well-being, a group of church leaders discussed how they might be of more help to her. "I know what it's like in a strange land," said one former missionary. "Missionaries have special problems. Could we agree to pray specifically for some of those needs? Things like coping with a strange culture, the physical problems of living in the tropics, and maintaining good relationships with other missionaries."

The church leaders envisioned themselves in Jenny's place, thinking about the particular problems she might face. Each then agreed to pray for Jenny concerning one of these problems.

When the church leaders received their first letter from Jenny, they found that each day she had a grueling uphill climb to a mountain village where she worked all day until she came back down at sunset. Jenny said she had struggled up the mountain each day wondering how she could keep going. Then she received a letter from the church leaders reassuring her of their prayers.

Jenny felt blessed to know that people were praying for her specific needs. Her work became less of a strain, the tiredness left her body, and she could virtually run down the mountainside at the end of the day.

Jenny told them how she felt the presence of God in her work, and she knew that their prayers had made the difference. The church had

spoken in the name of Jesus, and one more person had been strengthened by God's grace.

In what ways did the prayers of her church benefit Jenny?

_____

_____

_____

_____

List as many factors as you can that led to the healing of the lame man
at the Beautiful Gate.

_____

_____

_____

_____

In what way will you act within the authority you have as a Christian
disciple to bring God's healing/reconciling/supporting power to
bear on the life of someone this coming week?

_____

_____

_____

_____

Describe a situation in which God's healing power was brought to
bear upon the life of an individual.

_____

_____

_____

15

Holiness, Not Happiness Alone

Many Christian disciples do not want to be thought of as holy. "Holy Joe" is usually understood to be a person who is so heavenly-minded that he is of no earthly good.

Rather than separating himself from the world in a cocoon of superficial piety, the Christian disciple must be willing to get his hands dirty in the work of the world. That does not mean that God wants us to walk about with one foot in heaven and one in hell as we try to be "one of the gang." He calls us to a true holiness through a purging and sanctifying process which day by day sharpens us into the likeness of Christ.

Paul deals with this issue in Ephesians 4:17-24.

Paul asks his followers to give up the old pagan ways. The pagan does not understand the very purpose of life and is therefore condemned to a life of ignorance, of separation from God, of blindness of heart. Insensitive to feelings, the pagan gives his life to vice, stopping at nothing to satisfy his evil desires. His lack of purpose locks him in.

By way of contrast, Paul then talks about the Christian life. The Christian thinks and acts from the truth that is in Jesus Christ. Man was created in the image of God, but it is only in Christ that we can see the image of God which God intended man to see. To "learn Christ" means a great deal more than acquiring knowledge about Him. It is allowing that knowledge to change our lives, enrich our minds, move our hearts, and guide our wills.

To "learn Christ" the Christian puts off the old man (his former nature), and turns his back on those thoughts and deeds that were a part of his old nature. He becomes a new man in Christ, new in mind and spirit.

Paul does not say that this is an easy process, but it is the one to which we are called. When we allow Christ to become a living truth within us, He becomes our life. Holiness becomes not so much an ideal to work toward, but a second nature to our life in Christ.

Father Andrew once returned by ship from South Africa with a man who was seeking holiness.[15] At first, the man seemed reluctant to share with the English monk the real concern of his heart. At length he said, "I wish with my whole heart that I had your faith. I am not what the world would call an unhappy man. I am quite well off. But I cannot see the use of life, and I can say with certainty that if this life were offered to me now and I could take it or leave it I would most certainly leave it. I cannot see its purpose or its meaning or its worth. I only wish I had your faith and could make something of it."

So much depends upon a person's view of life. If life is looked upon primarily for the pleasure it may bring, it will bring boredom. There is no sense of permanence to life and no concept of holiness, for there is no reason why life should be permanent if it is not precious and holy. The end of life is not happiness but holiness.

According to Father Andrew, life exists for the creation of character, and character is formed by the choices we make. Character is enriched as we choose by faith that which will purify the soul. We sacrifice earthly pleasure for a vision of holiness. The man on the ship with Father Andrew wanted holiness, and he had seen that the pleasures of the world could not bring him that satisfaction. Only when the old ways were set aside and the new man born through Christ could the way to holiness be attained.

From reading the passage in Ephesians what do you understand "holiness" to be?

_____

_____

_____

Why had the man on the ship never discovered true holiness?

_____

_____

_____

_____

What area of your life needs purging in the coming week? What are you going to do about it?

_____

_____

_____

_____

How would you have handled the discussion with the man on the ship if he had come to you instead of to Father Andrew?

_____

_____

_____

_____

16

Suffering for Others

When our loved ones face suffering and trouble, we want to bear that suffering for them. That is a natural desire experienced by non-Christians as well as Christians.

However, the Christian disciple is called to step beyond this and be willing to suffer for someone he may not like, for someone he may not even know.

I have often wondered if I would be willing to jump in front of a speeding car to push another person to safety. Could I perform other acts of self-sacrifice in dangerous situations? The Lord has guided me to a realization that few of us have opportunities for heroic self-sacrifice. But if, in the routines of our daily lives, we look about us, we will see many opportunities to suffer for others. We often have the opportunity, for instance, to fast and pray sacrificially for others.

In any situation, the crux of the matter is the desire of our hearts. Are we willing to be Christ's disciples in mundane ways as well as in dramatic, life-risking moments that will probably never occur?

Read Luke 23:1-12.

The charges brought against Jesus were clearly trumped up. He was accused of the very thing He refused to claim: of being a king in the worldly sense. The evidence consisted of outright lies and intentional misunderstandings. The chief priests knew that Jesus had not claimed to be "Christ a king" in the sense in which they hoped Pontius Pilate would understand it. They wanted Pilate to believe

Jesus to be a revolutionary stirring up trouble for his not-too-effective Roman rule over the Jewish people.

Pilate was not fooled. He knew that the Jewish leaders had set Jesus up on false charges, and he told them so.

That should have been the end of the matter, but Pilate was not a man of strong character. When he realized that Jesus was from Galilee, he saw the opportunity to shift responsibility to the Galilean governor, Herod, who was in Jerusalem at the time.

Jesus went before Herod, who knew about Jesus and wanted to use Him for his own benefit, to see some miracle performed or otherwise to be amused. Jesus responded with silence. Herod made a joke of the whole affair and allowed his soldiers to dress Jesus in royal garments, mock, and abuse Him.

What a sick joke it was! Two weaklings who were supposed to be leaders failed to exercise proper authority or to administer justice. In their midst stood Jesus—silent, confident, and with the real authority that Herod and Pilate lacked utterly. They made sport of Him and professed to pass judgment. Their actions, in truth, only condemned themselves.

Whenever one person must suffer for the sins of another, there Jesus stands sharing the pain and transforming it into glory.

John and Karen Howe tell of an incident that occurred at a boys' summer camp some years ago.[16] One of the youngsters had broken every rule in the book. He misbehaved so badly that he made life miserable for the staff and for the rest of the campers.

The problem boy had come from a bad home situation; so sending him back home didn't seem to be the solution. It would have made things worse for the boy and evidenced failure on the part of the camp.

The boy had lied, stolen, torn up equipment, bullied younger campers, and done many other things. What could be done?

The head counselor called his staff together and brought the boy before them. "You deserve to be whipped," he told the boy; and then he added, "but I will take it for you." He stooped over and allowed one of the counselors to give him the whipping that the boy deserved.

The boy watched in shock and then began to cry. For a long time he cried uncontrollably. When he stopped, he was a different person. The whipping, had he received it himself, might have made him even more hostile to those around him. Seeing someone else suffer in his place, however, broke his heart.

Jesus did that for us all.

In the story of the boys' camp, how do you think the following felt about the whipping administered to the head counselor: (a) the boy who deserved the whipping; (b) the head counselor; (c) the one who administered the whipping; (d) the spectators?

_____

_____

_____

_____

Why did Jesus refuse to answer the questions of Pilate and Herod?

_____

_____

_____

_____

What opportunity will you have in the coming week to suffer for another? How will you do it?

_____

_____

_____

_____

What experience have you had in suffering for someone else? How did you feel about it at the time?

_____

_____

_____

_____

17

Dealing with Resentment

Forgiveness is like patience; we need a lot of grace to perfect either of them.

There are multitudes of Christians who do not realize that in their unforgiving, resentful attitudes they are sinning. Christian disciples should forgive quickly. Not only does God expect us to be forgiving; we cannot minister effectively in Christ's name if we are burdened with resentments.

Peter raised the question about forgiveness, and in Matthew 18:21-35 our Lord dealt clearly with the issue.

Despite his human failings, Peter was the chief of the apostles, and when he spoke there was always some important lesson to be learned.

He asked if it was sufficient to forgive a person "seven times." He was willing to be generous, to have an attitude of forgiveness, but there were limits to his forgiveness.

Jesus said that we are to forgive "seventy times seven." We should forgive always with no strings attached. We are to forgive as often as necessary, as often as there is anything to forgive. Peter was thinking of the sinfulness of the person who did wrong; Jesus thought of the sinfulness of the person who failed to forgive.

To illustrate His point, Jesus told a parable. A man of power and position forgave his servant an extremely large debt when the servant begged for mercy. After he had been forgiven, however, the servant refused to forgive a much smaller debt owed to him by another. We are to consider why someone who has experienced in abundance the grace of God can treat another unmercifully. One who fails to forgive can expect only strict judgment for his own sins.

God's continual forgiveness and mercy are reason enough for us to show mercy and forgiveness to others. If we cannot see forgiveness in that positive light, the parable of Jesus gives us an alternative: we can expect severe judgment for our lack of forgiveness. The unforgiving have no place in heaven, where mercy is both a requirement for entry and the central theme of existence.

Larry Christenson tells a story of forgiveness.[17] Following the death of her husband, a woman had raised her daughter virtually single-handed. She had made great sacrifices for the girl's well-being. When the girl ran off and got married without her permission, the mother was distraught.

The woman's first reaction was resentment. How could the daughter be so thankless? Then the woman began to question her own relationship with God. She had been a prayerful person, but now she knew she was out of contact with God. In her despair, she went to a clergyman and said, "You've got to do something. I can't find God." He talked with her and encouraged her to turn over her resentment to the Lord.

As she prayed, the woman came to see the power of forgiveness in Christ, especially the power of Christ's blood to cleanse away sin. She said it was as if God had come in with a giant vacuum cleaner and sucked all the resentment out of her.

She also came to a greater understanding of the nature of resentment and forgiveness. First of all, she learned that resentment was sin on her part. What the daughter had done was primarily between the daughter and God. The mother's resentment of the daughter's action was sin; judgment was God's business, not hers.

Then she had further insight: you don't lose your peace with God over someone else's sin, only over your own. People did terrible things to Jesus, but He never reacted with resentment, and He never lost His peace with God. The acts committed against Him were not problems to Him; they lay between God and the people who committed them.

Jesus simply forgave, and that is the way He expects us to live.

Did the mother in the story have a right to expect better treatment from her dauthter? Why wasn't she justified in resenting the treatment she received?

_____

_____

_____

_____

Why did Jesus use a parable to illustrate His attitude toward forgiveness?

_____

_____

_____

_____

Whom should you forgive this week? How will you go about it? (Be careful never to confront a person with your need to forgive him. This will create a greater offense. If the person hasn't sought your forgiveness, it will be better to express your forgiveness to God in prayer.)

_____

_____

_____

_____

Think of a time when you were forgiven for a sin of great consequence. How did you feel?

_____

_____

_____

18

What Christians Are Like

In the first part of our study of discipleship, we considered five of the fruits of the Spirit listed in Galatians 5:22-23. In the following chapters, we will look at the remaining fruits: goodness, faithfulness, gentleness, and self-control.

Goodness, as seen by Paul, is concerned with ideal character: righteousness softened by love. That sounds like a definition of Jesus; therefore, it is difficult to find a Bible passage or a story to illustrate goodness adequately. Dr. William Barclay says that the supreme message of the New Testament is not that Jesus is like God, but that God is like Jesus. We must look at the New Testament in its entirety to see a complete picture of goodness.

But there is a Gospel story that goes to the heart of Jesus' character which tells us something of goodness. It is found in John 13:12-17.

When He washed the disciples' feet, Jesus acted out a parable and told a story with deeper meaning than may have appeared to them at the time.

By washing the disciples' feet, Jesus demonstrated the nature of His royal identity and, at the same time, gave His disciples an example to follow.

It was not enough for the twelve to recognize Jesus as their Master; they must express their love for Him in their love for others. It is so with every Christian. As Jesus was in perfect obedience to His Father, we should be in obedience to Christ. We are not called simply to think out our faith, but to manifest goodness.

How do we put goodness into practice? Sometimes it will mean speaking for Jesus in answer to someone's particular need. At other times it will mean acting for Jesus when speaking won't help. Always it will mean living for Jesus; our lives are the clearest evidence of our faith.

If we call ourselves Christians, let us in our generation be Christ to our neighbor and to all around us. Through the guidance of God's Holy Spirit, we can.

What Christians are like is illustrated by Stephen Verney's story of an African girl.[18]

Maria lived in Angola in West Africa, and she was always laughing. One day the Anglican missionaries were discussing evangelism. This involved various methods including pamphlets, missions, and campaigns.

After a while, someone turned to Maria. "What do you do in your church, Maria?'

"In my church," said Maria, "we don't give pamphlets to people or have missions. We just send one or two Christian families to live in a village, and when people see what Christians are like, they want to be Christians themselves."

Can there be a more eloquent testimony than that?

God has sent us into our particular neighborhoods in the same way Maria's church sends Christians into the villages. Do the results of our lives match Maria's expectations? Why? Why not?

_____

_____

_____

_____

How was the goodness of Jesus demonstrated when He washed His disciples' feet?

_____

_____

_____

In what ways during the coming week can you show forth the goodness that is a fruit of the Spirit?

_____

_____

_____

_____

Has anyone ever offered to "wash your feet?" What were the circumstances? How did you react and why?

_____

_____

_____

_____

19

Barnabas

Faithfulness is the fruit of the Spirit which we will consider next. To Paul, the term apparently meant fidelity to other human beings.

In our studies thus far we have seen instances of fidelity, but here we are to focus on a particular characteristic. How is the Christian disciple to regard his fellow-man, and to what extent should he vouch for another, even when it means difficulty for himself?

Read Acts 9:26-31.

The story illustrates the fidelity of Barnabas to Paul. To the apostles in Jerusalem, Paul was a notorious character. It was in Jerusalem that Paul had persecuted Christians, and it was difficult for the apostles to believe that he was now one of them. It was natural for them to suspect that he was a secret agent who would use his new information to wreak greater havoc upon the Church.

Barnabas, however, was willing to take the risk. He not only defended Paul, he brought him into the midst of the apostles. He told them of Paul's experience on the Damascus road and his conversion to Christianity. He told them that Paul had preached boldly in the name of Jesus, that he had faced death for his faith. It was only then that the apostles accepted Paul and put him to work among them.

Barnabas' actions tell us something about his character. He believed the best of others. In that regard, he followed the example of our Lord. Jesus often chose unpopular people for His associates.

Barnabas also showed that he was forgiving. It would have been easy to resent Paul for the harm he had done the church, and

Barnabas undoubtedly knew people who had suffered at Paul's hands. But, again, he followed the example of our Lord who forgave "seventy times seven."

We can thank God for Barnabas and the part he played in bringing Paul into the company of the apostles. Perhaps the rich blessing of Paul would have been lost had it not been for the faithfulness of Barnabas.

In our own time, there is a parallel to the story of Paul and Barnabas in the story of a handful of men who supported Charles Colson when he was one of the most unpopular men in the nation.[19] Colson had been a right-hand man for President Nixon during the time of the Watergate scandal, and most Americans were convinced that he was guilty of many misdeeds.

During the Watergate crisis, Colson experienced a genuine Christian conversion. Shortly afterwards, several prominent politicians began to meet regularly with Colson as brothers in Christ. They were men whose political philosophies differed radically from Colson's; yet, in the Lord they were one.

Initially, few people knew that men of the stature of Senator Harold Hughes were willing to meet openly with Colson. But the men who formed the weekly prayer group with Colson did not hide their connection with him. They risked their political reputations to support a brother in need.

In the ensuing months and years, untold sacrifices of time and energy were expended by these men on Colson's behalf. When the time came, they traveled miles to visit him in prison. One of them uncovered an old law which allowed one person to serve a prison sentence for another, and volunteered to complete Colson's term for him.

That kind of faithfulness cannot be explained outside a context of Christian love.

How can we achieve a sense of brotherhood and loyalty for someone with a political philosophy opposed to our own?

_____

_____

_____

Find in the Bible another example of Barnabas' faithfulness. Compare it with the example used in this chapter.

_____

_____

_____

_____

How, in the coming week, can you show the fruit of faithfulness?

_____

_____

_____

_____

Recall an instance in your past when you showed, or failed to show, faithfulness like that of Barnabas. How did you feel?

_____

_____

_____

_____

20

Reaching Out in Compassion

Gentleness, another fruit of the Spirit, should be manifested in the life of a Christian disciple.

In its purest form, as seen by Paul, gentleness reflects submission to God's will as well as consideration for one's fellow-men.

To keep a proper balance between obedience to God and compassion for mankind sounds very much like "Love the Lord your God with all your heart and soul and mind, and your neighbor as yourself." Gentleness is what God expects of us as we fulfill His commandment.

Read Luke 18:15-16.

In this brief passage, we see that women had brought their children to Jesus that He might touch them. In trying to understand the reaction of the disciples, it is important to remember that not only children but women themselves were relatively insignificant in the Jewish world of Jesus' time. It was a bold step for the women to come into Jesus' presence, and bolder still for them to bring their children to Him.

The disciples scolded them for their presumption and tried to drive them away. It would be interesting to know exactly what they said. Did they argue that the Master was too busy, or didn't have the time, or that He had better things to do than be sentimental over a few children?

The disciples may have felt the need to protect Jesus from those who sought Him constantly; they may have reflected the Jewish prejudices of the day against women and children. The result was the same: they were being exclusive. In their action they were not so unlike the Pharisees. They were separating themselves from others.

As individual Christians, and as Christ's church, we must be extremely careful not to be exclusive, not to separate ourselves and our Lord from those who are seeking and those who are in need. Jesus would not have it that way. He said, "Suffer little children to come unto me, and forbid them not."

In those simple words and in the words that follow, Jesus showed us His gentleness. He not only accepted the children and loved them, He used them as an example for us all. It is God's will that we have compassion for our fellows, even little fellows.

Helen Shoemaker tells about a disciple in our time whose response differed from that of the disciples in the Bible passage.[20] A young American woman had gone with her husband to a new African nation to participate in an American foreign-aid program. While there, she became very concerned about the African people among whom she lived and worked. She learned the language by going with a Peace Corps doctor to the villages in the "bush" once a week to care for mothers and children who were ill.

She became an interpreter for the group and helped care for sick babies who were brought to the doctor. One day a young mother dying of tuberculosis brought her baby in for treatment. The baby was being breast-fed by the mother and, although several months old, weighed only eight pounds.

The child was seriously ill. What was the young American woman to do? There was no hospital equipped to take the dying mother and baby, so the young woman volunteered to care for the baby in her own home. She had not been well herself, having contracted a parasitic disease common in Africa; but she reached out in compassion to a woman and child in need. She was a listening Christian, and she knew she was doing what Jesus wanted her to do.

She took the child into her home, and nursed him back to health in four months' time. Because the mother had died, the woman then placed the baby with a childless African couple who wanted to adopt him. God protected her health and allowed her to save the life of a small, helpless, dying baby.

Once again, as it has happened down through the centuries, a Christian servant was given the privilege of reaching out in compassion and thereby was drawn nearer to her Lord.

How many people benefited from the gentleness of the disciple in the African story? Who were they? What was the effect upon each of them?

_____

_____

_____

_____

Why did Jesus use little children for an example to His disciples?

_____

_____

_____

_____

In the coming week, how can you exercise the spiritual fruit of gentleness?

_____

_____

_____

_____

Think of an instance when you have experienced gentleness from another. What was the result?

_____

_____

_____

_____

21

Temple of the Holy Spirit

Self-control is the last fruit of the Spirit which we will consider here. It is manifested in an ability to restrain our carnal impulses. It is a characteristic desperately needed in the hedonistic world in which we live today.

It is often said that the "new morality" is really the old immorality; and that is, unfortunately, true. Recently I was discussing premarital counseling with a clergyman who began his remarks by saying, "When I counsel a couple who are ready to be married and who are not already living together . . .". We live in a world more and more bereft of the sense of moral responsibility.

Even Christians make the serious mistake of assuming that the world's ways are more "practical" (and therefore acceptable) than God's ways as they are defined in the Bible. But what seems practical in the short run can be disastrously impractical in the long run. We can see but a short distance ahead; God foresees the whole story. Read 1 Corinthians 6:12-20.

Dr. William Barclay translates verse 12 as "True, all things are allowed to me; but all things are not good for me. All things are allowed to me, but I will not allow anything to get control of me."[21]

Paul here used meat as a specific illustration, but his real concern was with sexual purity. He did not consider the body in its physical sense alone. To him, the body included the entire personality. A person who understands sexuality only as the satisfaction of physical appetites has a narrow view, indeed.

In Paul's day, the world saw the needs and actions of the body as irrelevant to the spiritual life. It is much the same today. Paul opposed this view. To him, the body was not a temporary shelter for the soul; it was to be renewed in a form worthy of a place in the Kingdom of God. Our resurrected body must bear some resemblance to our earthly body. The resurrection of Christians is in the likeness of the resurrection of Christ.

Fornication with a harlot broke the union between Christ and the Christian, for in Paul's day, a temple prostitute was in the service of a pagan god. A Christian could not be joined to a harlot and also to the Lord. It was a moral and religious impossibility.

Fornication in any age and with any other person is a degradation of bodies and souls which should serve the Lord with higher and happier purpose.

Paul developed his argument step by step. "Flee fornication," he said. Don't even get close to the temptation. Mere disapproval is not enough; we must stay away from it altogether.

Paul goes to the heart of the matter. As Christians, our bodies are temples of the Holy Spirit. In a sense, they are no longer ours, but exist to glorify God. We are reminded of the price Christ paid on the cross to make us His. And we are not only to refrain from immorality; we are to make our whole bodies (flesh and spirit) available for God's service.

I have come to a vivid realization of these verses as a result of my own personal experiences. In my pre-Christian years I was often obsessed with sexual desires. Even in my early Christian years, I accepted the world's view that a few dirty books and movies "weren't all that bad." Sex was normal, and we didn't want to get Puritanical about it, did we?

Fortunately for me, our adult Sunday school class had some honest discussions about this matter. Using as a guide William Law's, *A Serious Call to a Devout and Holy Life,* we found some practical help in Holy Scripture. For one thing, we learned that in addition to "fleeing fornication," it was a good idea to stay away from books, movies, and magazines which stimulate sexual desires.

I do not doubt that much of what we are is shaped by the books, the movies and television, and the conversation to which we expose ourselves. When I stayed away from dirty jokes and erotic movies and literature, my sexual temptations diminished.

We seldom give the Bible credit for being a practical guidebook, but God's reasons for sexual purity are found in the words of many verses in Holy Scripture. They reveal depths of meaning and principles by which we can live.

Is it true that we become what we read? Support your opinion with examples.

_____

_____

_____

_____

What are the main points of Paul's arguments against fornication?

_____

_____

_____

_____

What area of your life (an area which has nothing to do with sexual impurity) must be changed because it shows a disregard of your body as a temple of the Holy Spirit? What are you going to do about it?

_____

_____

_____

_____

Recall an incident in your past in which you made the wrong moral decision because you were persuaded by the world, the flesh, or the devil, and not by God's word.

_____

_____

_____

_____

22

The Old Well

We have considered all nine of the fruits of the Spirit listed by Paul in Galatians 5:22-23. As we grow in discipleship, we should manifest these fruits in our lives. However, it is important to realize that the fruits are not things we do, but rather something we hope to have.

It is not that, as Christians, we decide that we must be gentle then grit our teeth and go forth to be gentle. By listing the fruit, Paul does not give us a command, but a checklist. We can check the list, and if God's grace is not being manifested in our lives we will know that something is wrong. We will know that something has clogged the channel between God and us, because His grace is not flowing through us to the world.

Read John 7:37-52.

The passage seems to be a strange statement from Christ producing very mixed reactions from people who heard Him.

When Jesus spoke, it was the last day of the Feast of the Tabernacles, a major event in the Jewish year. On the first seven days of the Feast, water from the pool of Siloam was carried to the Temple in remembrance of God's gift of water from the rock in Moses' time. On the eighth day, to recall Israel's entrance into the land of springs of water, the water was not taken to the Temple.

The prophet Zechariah had foretold a day when living waters from Jerusalem would bring life to all around, and at the Feast of Tabernacles there was a high degree of expectation that the prophecy would be fulfilled.

"In the last day, that great day of the feast," Jesus said, "if any man thirst, let him come unto me, and drink." He said that the prophecy was being fulfilled in Him, that not only will everyone who comes to Him to drink be filled with the living water, but he will also become a fountain from which others may drink.

Then we see the different reactions to what Jesus has said:

1. The common people appeared to be deeply impressed. Some said He is a prophet who would announce the coming of the Messiah, the promised Savior sent by God.

2. Other common people believed that Jesus was the Messiah Himself, the Christ.

3. The remainder of the common people were confused because they could not fit Jesus into their traditional beliefs about the Messiah.

4. Next, we see the reaction of the Temple police, men who were trained to obey orders rather than to think for themselves. Yet, they were dumbfounded by the authority with which Jesus spoke, and they failed to arrest Him.

5. The Pharisees, the pious Jewish leaders of the day, closed their minds. They were satisfied with their own beliefs and wanted nothing to do with Truth that might challenge those beliefs.

6. Finally, there was Nicodemus, a man who had seen the wonder of Jesus and wanted to know more; but he was silenced quickly by the Pharisees.

Jesus had spoken a great truth that acceptance of Him could change a person so completely that the power and love of God would be in him and flow through him to others, like "living water." As we see in our own day, some accept, some reject the claims of Jesus.

John Sanford learned a truth about "living water" when he was a boy visiting his family's summer place in New Hampshire. His father was a clergyman and the family was short of money, so they lived in the 150-year-old farmhouse quite simply, without the modern conveniences of today.

The water supply during those years came from an old well which stood just outside the front door. The water was especially cold and pure, and the well never ran dry. Even in the worst periods of summer drought, the old well produced its cool, pure water.

Later the Sanfords were able to improve the house, adding modern plumbing, including a deep artesian well drilled several hundred feet from the house. The old well was sealed over, to be kept in reserve only if, for some unforeseen reason, the new artesian well should fail.

One day, John Sanford's curiosity got the best of him, and he uncovered the old well to see how it was doing. To his great surprise, he found that it had gone bone dry.

Why? Because a well of that kind is fed by hundreds of small underground rivulets through which a constant supply of water seeps. When water is removed from the well, more water seeps along the rivulets, keeping them constantly open. But when a well is not used for a long period of time, the rivulets close up. The well went dry because it had not been used.

So it is with the "living water" that comes from Christ. If we practice our faith and let God's love and power flow through us, we continue to be wellsprings of "living water." But if we do not follow the teachings of Jesus, we, too, may dry up like the old well and be of no use to anybody.

Compare John Sanford's feelings on finding the old well dry with our own feelings when we discover that we have "gone dry" spiritually.

_____

_____

_____

_____

Compare the reactions of the people who heard Christ's teaching to the reactions of people today to the teachings of Christ.

_____

_____

_____

_____

What has been blocking the flow of living water in your life, and what can you do about it?

_____

_____

_____

_____

Think of a truth you discovered when you were a child which was later confirmed for you through Holy Scripture.

_____

_____

_____

_____

23

My Help Cometh

We are not immune from the pressures of the world even though we are disciples of Christ. Although by God's grace we have strength and guidance which non-Christians lack, we still have our share of problems. We can become discouraged and feel defeated.

During periods of depression and doubt, many Christians find great comfort in the Psalms. Their honesty—sometimes raw honesty—teaches us to be straightforward in our approach to God. Yet, the Psalms also demonstrate a great reverence for God and a deep sense of worship.

But most of all in the Psalms we find reassurance of God's love and protection. Read Psalm 121.

Reading between the lines of this psalm, we sense a feeling of uncertainty, but still the writer puts his trust in God. A perilous journey seems to lie before him, and yet he looks to the Lord for the strength and guidance which he will need.

Perhaps the goal of his pilgrimage is in the mountains, perhaps even Mt. Zion, the mount of God. But he knows he will be protected, and help will come from God.

The God of Israel can be counted upon. He has proved Himself throughout the history of His chosen people. The repetition of "neither slumber nor sleep" underlines the certainty of the claim. The Keeper of Israel protects the traveler from his adversaries night and day.

Finally, the protection is from "all evil," from every kind of trouble throughout life forever. That is quite an insurance policy.

Some years ago I was facing a "perilous journey"; at least, it seemed so to me, and I did not feel well equipped as a Christian disciple. I had been in New Mexico for a church meeting and I was ready to begin my journey home the next morning, feeling rejected and very lonely.

I had been invited to the meeting as the keynote speaker. A dual assignment had been given to me, to give an entertaining talk and at the same time present a Bible study program for adoption by the group, representing some fifty churches.

Originally, the talk was to have lasted approximately 45 minutes. As the moment to speak drew near, the time was cut to 30 minutes. Then, right before I got up to address the several hundred people in attendance, I was asked to speak no more than 20 minutes.

By God's grace, I was able to say all that I needed to say in that brief period, and I felt good about the reception I was given. Many people were very interested in the Bible study program, and I was enthusiastic about its use in their churches. But then, on the final day of the meeting, they decided to take a vote on approval of the program, and the program was accepted by the narrowest of margins.

As I sat, alone, in the motel restaurant following the meeting, I felt sorry for myself. The memory of that close vote still rankled me, but much more than that, I dreaded the trip ahead. The next day I would be stopping in Memphis to visit my brother who, at 45 and the father of four, was dying of cancer.

It was selfish to be thinking of myself, but everything seemed so unfair. Somehow I needed to get my brother, who had not been a regular churchgoer, into the care of a church that could minister to his needs in his time of travail. I was only going to have a brief stay in Memphis, however, and it would take a miracle to accomplish what seemed to be needed.

To top it all off, as I sat there in the restaurant in my bone-weary and self-pitying state, I knew I could not have even a glass of wine because of the commitment I had made to the Lord not to drink alcoholic beverages. I got angry. "It's just not fair," I told the Lord, and I meant it!

Then, in His gracious goodness, it was as though the Lord took me in His arms and assured me that everything would be all right. I was filled with a euphoric feeling, and as I raised my eyes from the table I suddenly noticed the majestic mountains as the rays of the evening sun reflected upon them high above me.

The next morning, the selection in my daily devotional was Psalm 121.

Later that day, I found my brother willing to go with me to a church where faithful clergy and lay people ministered to him during his remaining days. Although he was not healed from the physical effects of his illness, he came into a close relation with the Lord and evangelized others from his death bed.

Why is it not sacrilegious to become angry with God?

_____

_____

_____

_____

What Psalms do you feel are a great source of comfort in time of trouble, need, and stress?

_____

_____

_____

_____

What have you been harboring within yourself about which you need to be honest with God?

_____

_____

_____

Have you ever been angry with God and let Him know it? What happened?

_____

_____

_____

_____

24

The Absence of God

There are times when Christian disciples become angry with God, and there are times when they feel that He has deserted them altogether.

On the subject of God's absence from us, there are at least two schools of thought. On the one hand, there is the old saw, "If you are not feeling close to God, guess who moved?" It says that it is always man who is responsible for separation from God.

On the other hand, there have been spiritual leaders through the ages who have believed that God sometimes withdraws from us, in a manner of speaking, so that we will grow. Separation from Him tests our faith in a special way. There is another old saying that "Fruit grows in the valley, not on the mountain top."

Jesus Himself endured separation from God, as we read in Mark 15:33-41.

Here was Jesus' agony at its deepest level. To those who loved Him, His failure must have appeared complete. He was no longer surrounded by those who mocked and scorned Him, but He must have felt utterly alone.

Jesus was crucified at the third hour (9 A.M.). From the sixth hour (noon) until 3 P.M., "There was a darkness over the whole land," the darkness of sin. Then, Mark records, a strange cry came from Jesus' lips: "My God, My God, why hast Thou forsaken Me?"

Was it a forlorn cry of separation from God? The line is from Psalm

22, and some think we should see it in the light of the entire psalm which resounds with trust and praise.

It is more likely that it expresses the price Jesus paid to be the Savior of the world. We cannot bear sin lightly, for it separates us from God. Jesus willingly bore the burden of the sin of the world and experienced, however momentarily, the agony of separation from God which we all experience from time to time.

But when He reached those depths, the victory was won. The reign of sin was broken and evil was overcome. Man was free. Jesus had opened for us a clear pathway to God.

Yet, still, from time to time, we find ourselves separated from God. Cecil B. Murphey tells how he lived through a time when he was separated from God.[23]

For a period of several months, Murphey's life had felt like a vacuum. He was unwilling to admit to others that God had "deserted him," and he was not willing to admit to himself that he was praying out of habit rather than from an awareness of God's presence.

One winter afternoon, as he walked through the snow and ice between the train station and his home, he talked to God. "Lord, you used to assure me of your presence. When I prayed, or read the Bible, or went to church, something happened inside of me—I felt alive! For months now, my heart has been as cold as this weather."

As he complained of "God's behavior," Murphey realized that God is with us even when we are not conscious of His presence. He remembered Isaiah 45:15: "Verily Thou art a God that hidest Thyself, O God of Israel, the Saviour."

At that moment, Murphey resolved to change his attitude. "God, even if you never again give me any visible evidence, I am still with you. Job said that he would trust you even if you killed him. I am determined to do the same."

As Murphey continued walking, the dark clouds rolled away, and the sun broke through for the first time that day. And, once more, the warmth of God's love broke into Murphey's life.

How do you think it must have felt to be the Son of God dying on a cross, rejected and condemned by a world you came to save?

_____

_____

_____

_____

What was the "key" that unlocked the door that separated Murphey from God?

_____

_____

_____

_____

Under what circumstances and in what ways have you felt separated from God? What was the "key" to your problem?

_____

_____

_____

_____

When, and for how long and crucial a period of time, have you felt separated from God? How was the problem resolved?

_____

_____

_____

_____

25

Opening Holy Scripture

"All scripture is given by inspiration of God, and is profitable for doctrine, for reproof, for correction, for instruction in righteousness." So says Second Timothy 3:16.

The study of the Bible is essential for the Christian disciple. We know God through worship, prayer, the teachings of the Church, through fellowship with other Christians, by doing God's work in the world, and in many other ways.

However, we best know God through daily contact with Holy Scripture. By studying the Bible day by day and letting God speak to us through His Living Word, we come, more and more, to have the mind of Christ.

It was that conviction that led me some years ago to establish the Bible Reading Fellowship in the United States. BRF is a program of daily Bible study that leads a disciple through the entire Bible every five years. It does this by covering ten to fifteen verses every day and commenting upon them. Not only does the program develop disciplined Bible study, but it also leads the lay person to a better understanding of what God is saying in the Bible passage.

Several months ago, the Bible Reading Fellowship came to an important crossroad. We were considering a major step forward that would require a commitment of time and funding. We had prayed, but we still were uneasy and wanted assurance from God that we were moving within His will.

The Board of Directors is composed of very busy people, some of whom come from long distances for the meetings. For their sakes, we had always hurried through our business as quickly as possible. But for this meeting, the Board chairman decided that we should open with Bible study. We considered several Scripture passages to suit our purposes, but the chairman said, "No! That would be tying God's hands; let Him speak to us through the BRF passage for the day."

To begin the meeting, the chairman prayed that God would give us a message about the work of the Bible Reading Fellowship. Then we read the passage for the day: Nehemiah 7:73 - 8:12. Read it now.

The story is about the reading of Scripture to the people of Israel, and the effect that understanding Scripture had upon them.

You can imagine the joy our Board experienced in reading that passage. It was just the reaffirmation of our work that we needed, and it also demonstrated a useful method of daily Bible study. If we pray expectantly that God will speak to us through the passage of Scripture to be studied that day, there are amazing results. Sometimes the entire passage speaks to our needs, and other times only a word or phrase "jumps out" and gives us an insight into our problem or concern. Sometimes nothing in the passage seems to speak to my particular need, but it does often enough that I use this approach regularly. It works particularly well for families, or spouses, studying the Bible together.

In this chapter we have reversed our usual process and told the story before we commented on the Bible passage. Even without my story, however, the Bible passage is full of meaning.

Nehemiah, the sixteenth book of the Bible, continues the history of the Jewish people written in First and Second Chronicles and in Ezra. Nehemiah, the political leader for whom the book was named, shared with Ezra, the priest, the credit for the reconstruction of Jerusalem and the renewal of faith after the return from exile in Babylon.

It was a time of new beginnings for the Israelites, and the passage tells that the Law of Moses was read to them for the first time. Their reaction was intriguing. They rejoiced when they heard the Law and understood it, but as they heard it they were convicted of their sin. And so they wept for joy and for their wrongdoing.

Scripture, like the two-edged sword, cuts both ways. We rejoice as we hear God speak to us, and we grieve because our lives do not measure up to His love.

If the Chairman of the Board of the Bible Reading Fellowship had chosen a Bible passage to study at the meeting, what would have been an appropriate one to choose?

_____

_____

_____

_____

Imagine yourself in the crowd of Israelites hearing the Law of Moses for the first time. How do you think you would have reacted, and why?

_____

_____

_____

_____

Prepare a plan for daily Bible study for the next week. What portions of Scripture will you read? How will you approach the study?

_____

_____

_____

_____

Have there been instances when God has spoken meaningfully to you through Scripture? Tell about them.

_____

_____

_____

26

Healing Amidst Pain

Christian disciples are not immune to suffering. God changes attitudes far more than He changes circumstances. All suffer, but we hope that His grace will sustain us so that, in the midst of our pain, we will have victory.

There is good and bad news about the suffering, trials, and tribulations which Christians face. The bad news is that suffering hurts. There is no way to escape that, and only the person in pain knows how bad it is. The good news is that God will teach us in this school of life, and our pain and problems can authenticate our ministry. We can help others when we have experienced the pain which they bear.

Read Second Corinthians 12:1-10.

False apostles had been boasting of their spiritual experiences, and Paul makes it clear to the Corinthians that he has had his own share of them.

He begins the letter by telling of spiritual experiences of his own. His being caught up "to the third heaven" apparently was a unique awareness of the presence of God which Paul experienced some time after he encountered Christ on the road to Damascus. "The man in Christ" to whom he refers is himself.

This particular experience of Paul's is either one which cannot be explained (spiritual experiences often are of that nature), or one which he is not at liberty to reveal. Fortunately, we who read his letters today do not have to be convinced that Paul was a man who had many profound encounters with God.

The primary point of this passage, however, is that Paul does not wish to be overestimated because of his spiritual experiences. He wants the Corinthians to know that he, like them, must suffer weaknesses. His "thorn in the flesh" may well have been a disease or disorder resulting from the hardships of his journeys.

Despite Paul's fervent prayers, his illness was not removed. God gave him something greater: sufficient grace with which to bear his suffering. From a human point of view, Paul wished to be rid of his pain. From a spiritual point of view he welcomed it, for through it he understood that it is in our weakness that God's strength is made perfect. It was a constant reminder to Paul that what we are able to accomplish is through God and not because of our own strength. Paul's own pain also helped him identify with sufferers to whom he ministered.

Emily Gardiner Neal, whom the Lord has used in a healing ministry, has a testimony like Paul's.[24] For years, from the strength of her own good health, she preached that when people look for healing they must seek first the Kingdom of God. Seek God for Himself, she said, before you ask for His healing gifts. That, she knew, was the key to healing.

In her own perfect health, however, she felt presumptuous as she preached to those in pain. Then she suffered a spinal injury which kept her in constant pain for six years. From that time, she has never hesitated to ask those who seek healing to seek first the Kingdom of God.

"Although for years," she said, "there was no evidence of healing in my own body, I feel myself not less blessed, but more—for I have known God's grace in my life to an extent I never knew before, continually sustaining, enabling, empowering."

Mrs. Neal now truly can sympathize with those in great pain. She realizes that there are times when suffering is so great it is impossible to think of anything else. She also knows that in the times when pain eases, God, in our moment of surrender to Him, can perform His healing work.

With Paul, Mrs. Neal learned another truth about Christian suffering. Instead of feeling sorry for herself—"Why should this happen to

me?''—she has learned to say, "Why shouldn't this happen to me?"
All people are subject to pain; why should Christians be exempt?
Being a Christian is no assurance of a life free from suffering, but a
Christian has the means of overcoming suffering.
Whatever tragedy we face, we do not face it alone. Our Lord is
with us. In the midst of our pain, we know that we are walking a road
which He has walked before us. There is no pain we can face that will
equal His crucifixion. Yet, beyond the Cross the victory was His, and
we walk in the sure knowledge of that victory.

What does Mrs. Neal's story tell us about ourselves and the Christian
ministries to which God has called us?

_____

_____

_____

_____

There are several "messages" in the Bible passage to the Corinthians.
List them.

_____

_____

_____

_____

In what ways has the Lord trained you in the "school of life" for your
ministry or ministries?

_____

_____

_____

_____

Think of the greatest pain you have ever suffered. How have you learned (or can you learn) through that pain to minister to others?

_____

_____

_____

_____

27

Maintaining Balance

It is easy to be deceived, and many things appear to be different from the way they really are. In the Christian life there are many paradoxes. How does the Christian maintain his balance? How can he stand firm on the foundation of his faith in a world of shifting sands?

He is only human, and he is subject to temptations, distractions, and fears. So he recognizes the need to "stay on the track."

Read Luke 19:29-40 and 23:21.

The entry into Jerusalem was the climax of a long journey, and it was the beginning of the greatest drama the world has ever experienced.

Jesus rode the donkey in what appeared to be a deliberate enactment of the prophecy in Zechariah 9:9-10 which tells of a king who would enter the city on a donkey rather than on a warhorse or chariot. The donkey was the indication that the king's authority was derived from his ability to maintain peace instead of war.

Jesus' disciples, with many others, hailed His triumphant entry. Without subjugation by force or fear, they gave Him their obeisance.

Jesus' action was unexpected. The popular belief was that the Messiah would lead the forces of Israel and overthrow the military might of Rome. Many who had followed Jesus for the wrong reasons were troubled. Jesus approached Jerusalem with kingly dignity, but He was not misled by the cheers of the people. No one was as realistic as He, and He knew that suffering lay before Him.

The picture quickly changed. Jesus was not the kind of Messiah the people wanted, and they rejected Him. In a few days "Hosanna" became "Crucify Him!" The disciples moved from joy into paralyzing fear.

The particular application that needs to be dealt with here cannot be well illustrated by a story such as we have used in the other chapters. The Scripture passage reveals a disturbing truth that has been typified by stories it would be too painful—and of no use—for me to tell. That truth is that Christian disciples have feet of clay; and, if they do not become aware of their fallibility and do all they can to protect against the wiles of Satan, too often they will turn their backs on Christ as surely as did the fickle crowd in Jerusalem.

Well-respected Christian disciples have seriously impaired their effectiveness in numerous ways, such as appropriating funds to their selfish use, cheating on their income taxes, abandoning their families, and getting involved in various sex scandals. Would-be Christian disciples are certainly not immune to such outrageous behavior; in fact, they are especially subject to Satan's ire and had better be especially wary of his wily ways.

I have tried to find a common thread in these defections from allegiance to God. In most cases, it seems to me that the problem is similar to the one that the would-be followers of Jesus experienced during the last week of His life. The word that best sums it up is probably *selfishness.*

Some of the modern-day disciples who have fallen away were people who were serving themselves by serving God. Others spent too little time in looking to Him and too much attending to their own desires. Many had a problem of pride which they had never gotten out into the open and dealt with; pride gives Satan the widest door of all to walk into the soul of a person. Similar problems faced the zealots in Christ's time who followed Him only so long as it was profitable to them, met their selfish desires, or fed their national pride in wanting to overthrow the Roman rulers.

How careful we must be to check out our motives, to insure that we are truly following Christ and not our own selfish wants. There is such a delicate tightrope we walk in trying to serve Christ while the world, the flesh, and the devil are all around us.

We will make mistakes; after all, we are only human. The important thing is that, in our heart of hearts, our first priority is to love God.

Life is an incessant parade of fragile moments.
The strengths that lift us far above ourselves
Balance delicately along the line
That divides our wills between Him and us;
And the Dark One stalks there, crafty and cunning,
Persistent, resourceful, unmerciful!
How well he knows how to have us,
And when he does, we lose our equilibrium,
Crashing down in the shambles of our own foolishness.

To cope with the intricate maze we call life
We have devised so many games.
And we are but old children
Called so easily to play.
So the stage is set and the games are played
Over and over and over again.
And we so often lose!
Should it be strange that we grow weary
Of this long battle,
And retreat into the quiet comfort of our hollow shells?

How long a season can we hide?
He who called us first will call us forth again.
Timidly, we venture out once more;
And then begin to feel the armor of His love
Making us bolder as we go,
Until we face another fragile moment.

Mold us, Lord, of sterner stuff;
Help us to be strong.
Structurally, is clay enough
To move these feet along?

—HCG

What do you imagine were Jesus' thoughts and feelings as He rode into Jerusalem?

_____

_____

_____

_____

What temptations could cause a Christian to go astray, and how could he overcome them?

_____

_____

_____

_____

What steps can you take during the coming week to examine yourself and your motives so that in your heart of hearts your first priority is to love God?

_____

_____

_____

_____

Can you tell of an instance in which you were disappointed with yourself as a disciple of Christ, when you fell away from God? Why did it happen? What resulted?

_____

_____

_____

_____

28

Holy Boldness

Christian disciples are called to boldness in the Lord. This may mean taking a dramatic and unpopular stand on a vital issue. It can also mean simply speaking a word of faith when it would be easier to remain silent.

In my life as a Christian I have been called more often to make simple statements of allegiance to Christ than to take dramatic and unpopular stands. Many times every day we have opportunities to speak a word of hope to a spiritually starving world. Often it would be easier to remain silent, but Christ calls us to speak up with holy boldness.

Paul had many occasions to be bold. Read Ephesians 3:1-13.

The passage is a digression from the subject Paul has been pursuing. He mentions the Gentiles and is drawn off the track to speak of his commission to them.

Paul wrote the words in difficult circumstances. He was in prison, probably chained night and day to a Roman soldier. Still, in appalling captivity, he was free.

Circumstances would not prevent him from carrying out his commission to the Gentiles. We can imagine that he preached to those men who were chained to him. By this very letter we know that he wrote in that place about his faith. He did not despair; his faith burned brightly within him.

The heart of this passage is "the mystery," the divinely revealed truth that the Gentiles were to be the fellow heirs with the Jews in "the unsearchable riches of Christ." In a time of great difficulty and danger, Paul communicated that message with holy boldness.

The people of Coventry in England were called to holy boldness as they prepared for the consecration of their new cathedral. Stephen Verney tells the story.[25]

The Bishop of Coventry realized that people from all over the world would come to see the new cathedral which had been built beside the ruins of the ancient cathedral burned during the destruction of the city in World War II. People and nations from all over the world had contributed money, talents, and materials to the construction of the new cathedral.

Bishop Cuthbert Bardsley wondered what the people would find when they came to Coventry—a dull and ordinary church, or a church alive and attuned to the will of God? Would they find a converted people? The Bishop knew that a consecrated people was far more important than a consecrated cathedral.

Bishop Bardsley held a series of meetings throughout his diocese to convince his people that God was calling them to be a church filled with His love and His purpose. He talked about a converted people with the inner peace, joy, and love that only committed Christians can possess. At the end of each meeting, he asked the people to do something that Anglicans were not accustomed to do: to pray aloud, from their hearts and in their own words.

There was always an agonizing silence after the Bishop called for prayer. Then one brave person would pray, and the barriers would fall. Soon, all over the room, people prayed.

On one occasion, as Verney recalls, the Bishop prayed and Verney prayed, followed by a long, painful silence. Then the Bishop roared, "O God, forgive us our cowardice!" With that, a woman on the front row prayed, and others followed. After the meeting, the woman confessed that praying aloud had brought her a new sense of the reality of prayer.

In Coventry, a great thing began in a small way, and the people grew into a powerful fellowship of God's love. By the time the cathedral was consecrated, the people of Coventry were witnessing in holy boldness to the world.

Picture yourself as one of the people sitting silent after the Bishop of Coventry's request for spoken prayers. What is your rationalization for remaining silent? What are the real reasons for your silence?

_____

_____

_____

_____

How could Paul, in prison and facing death, write words of hope to others?

_____

_____

_____

_____

What aspects of your life show a lack of holy boldness? What can you do about it in the coming week?

_____

_____

_____

_____

Have you ever spoken out in holy boldness? Tell about it.

_____

_____

_____

_____

29

Not My Will, But Thine

The Lord has a right to expect obedience from us. In the crises of our lives, God puts us to tests of faith. We have two chances to pass the tests.

First, we say, "Yes, Father," and do what He has asked us to do. The second chance comes when we have failed to say yes. Even then, we can learn from our failure to do His will. We ask His forgiveness and determine to be obedient at the next opportunity.

The first chance is better than the second. Jesus was always obedient to the Father the first time. Read Luke 22:39-46.

In this powerful passage we see the cost of Jesus' discipleship. We see human nature at its very best. He desired to escape, but He was willing to stand firm.

Jesus' calmness during His trial and execution was the result of the battle He fought and won in the garden. He knew the trap was closing around Him and the disciples, and He cautioned them to pray for strength, but exhausted and at the hour of night when resistence is low, they fell asleep.

Jesus prayed alone.

It was a confident prayer, God was "Father." The coming sacrifice weighed heavily upon Jesus, but He was able to say, "Not my will, but Thine, be done." An angel appeared to Him and strengthened Him. The test was passed, and He went on to victory.

Dr. William Barclay has said that "Jesus is the one person who never disappoints those who set their hopes upon Him. He is the one person in whom the dream always comes true."[26]

Jesus always obeyed His Father's will. I do not.

I have a vivid memory of one time when I did not obey God.

I was living in a small town in the South where everyone knew everyone else. When a new supermarket opened in that town, one of the gimmicks to attract customers was the offer of a free helium-filled balloon with any purchase. I attended the opening, made my purchase, and wanted a balloon for my children.

A crowd of people gathered around the man filling balloons from a helium tank, and among them was a little black boy. His eyes were wide with anticipation as he waited patiently for his balloon. But we were not in line, and people kept crowding in and snatching away the balloons as they were filled. The little black boy, who had been there from the start, said nothing but became conspicuous by his continued presence.

Finally, the man filling the balloons, sweaty and cross from trying to keep up with the demand, tossed an uninflated balloon to the black child and said, "Here, boy, blow it up yourself."

God told me what to do, but I stood there silently as the little boy went away wiping the tears from his eyes.

What should I have done in the situation in the supermarket?

_____

_____

_____

_____

Why do we say that Christ's victory was won in the Garden of Gethsemane? Was not the real victory on the Cross?

_____

_____

_____

_____

How can you prepare yourself to respond in obedience to God's will when He calls you to act in a specific situation?

_____

_____

_____

_____

_____

Reflect on some of the ways in which God has asked you to obey Him. Was there a common factor in those situations?

_____

_____

_____

_____

_____

30

Diligence and Wisdom

Some Christian disciples have become spiritual butterflies, flitting from one church to another, from one conference to another, and between a multitude of books and devotional methods. They are not wise in their selection of spiritual disciplines; they are not diligent in the things they undertake.

God gave us minds which He expects us to use well. He has provided a number of ways in which we may know and serve Him. He wants us to seek His will wisely and follow it persistently as we grow in discipleship.

An abundance of God's wisdom is available for us in Holy Scripture. Read Second Peter 1:1-17.

Peter wrote to people who were familiar with certain beliefs popular in his day. Many regarded material things as evil and the world as corrupt. The only way to escape evil and become a part of the divine nature was to separate oneself from worldly existence. This was done through "knowledge" given to those who were accepted into several mystery religions existing at that time.

Corruption lies not in material things as such, Peter wrote, but in human lust. We contend with this through "knowledge" found in Jesus Christ who, while living a human life, gave us insight into God Himself. He gave us "exceeding great and precious promises" by which we become partakers of the divine nature.

Peter leads us, one by one, through the steps we must take before we can partake of divine nature. *Faith,* belief in God, is the cornerstone which must result in virtue. *Virtue* is the quality of character and attitude in Jesus Christ. In turn, we must have *knowledge* of the mind of Christ, and living out this knowledge requires *self-control* (temperance). That will necessitate *fortitude* (steadfastness, patience), the determination to stand fast with Jesus until the end. *Godliness,* recognition of our dependence upon God, is important and must be shown in *brotherly kindness,* the care and concern that should exist between Christian brothers and sisters and be a witness to the world around. Finally, there is *love,* the highest quality of the Christian life.

As he takes us through these steps, Peter demands of us diligence so that the wisdom we seek and the truth that is revealed to us may be deep and rich.

Dr. Charles Whiston calls for the same degree of diligence as he repeats a story of St. Francis de Sales.[27]

Harm, Dr. Whiston says, can come from reading too many books. There is the analogy of bees making honey.

During the late spring and early summer there is an abundance of flowers, but the bees do not make their best honey then. They flit from flower to flower, never going deep enough into the honey sacks. Later in the year when there are fewer flowers, the bees must dig deep into the flowers. It is then they produce the best honey.

So it can be with devotional study. If we read too many books and try too many methods of Bible study, we may never reach the real truths which God wishes us to find. It is when we select the best books and diligently use the best plan of study that we find the wisdom we desire.

List some ways in which Christians can be as fruitless as bees are at the height of the blooming season.

_____

_____

_____

_____

List those qualities necessary for sharing in the divine nature (from the Bible passage). Put *faith* at the bottom of the list and *love* at the top. Explain in your own words how each builds logically upon the one immediately beneath it.

_____

_____

_____

_____

_____

_____

_____

_____

How, during the next week, can you incorporate wisdom and diligence into your devotional life?

_____

_____

_____

_____

What, in your spiritual life, have been the most effective methods of growth?

_____

_____

_____

_____

31

Marvelous Things

On the wall behind my desk is a plaque which says, "God is subtle." Another old saying goes, "God is a gentleman; He never forces Himself on anyone."

The disciple of Christ learns to see God working in the world: I have seen and have experienced a number of miracles. I know, however, that a disbeliever could look at those miracles and, to his own satisfaction, disprove them all.

Most of the time, God works His miracles "naturally," but behind the natural phenomena, the follower of Christ can see the super-natural pattern of God's action. The disbeliever will not, or cannot, see God's subtle movements in the lives of His people.

Many of the Psalms are affirmations of God's work in the world. Read Psalm 98.

The psalm, a great song of praise, was composed for the Jewish Feast of Tabernacles, the primary feast of Kingship. It recalls the events of the Exodus in which the Israelites were granted salvation in the sight of the heathen.

An echo of God's promise in Isaiah 49:6 is found here. "I will also give thee (Israel) for a light to the Gentiles, that thou mayest be my salvation unto the end of the earth." God's salvation is worldwide.

Rejoice, the people are urged; consider the saving acts of God. There is cause for praise and thanksgiving; the Lord is King.

It is easy to join in the worship of this psalm. We are reminded that in a personal way, by "His right hand, and His holy arm," God does marvelous (miraculous, supernatural) things. He is faithful to his promises and to His people. He is in control.

We will see God performing miracles in our lives when we praise Him for His bountiful goodness and trust Him to continue to work His will in the world. Sometimes God's purposes are carried out in logical, everyday events; at other times there may be one unusual "coincidence" after another.

It has been my privilege to take part in a series of events which clearly revealed God working in the lives of His people.

The Church in Africa, despite great difficulties and cruel persecutions, is growing stronger every day. African Christians are now going out into the world to inspire and encourage the Christians in Europe and America.

I had been working for some time in my church to prepare for a visit from an African bishop and evangelist. During this time, I went to our National Church offices in New York for a meeting regarding an entirely different matter.

However, while I was there I heard the story of a young African whom I shall call "John." I was particularly interested in John's story, I am sure, because of the work I was doing for the African bishop.

John, the son of another bishop, had escaped from his native African country during savage persecutions of Christians there. He was safe but completely without resources and with no hope whatsoever of continuing his education in a highly specialized field. He had hoped to serve his people when his education was completed.

When I heard John's story, I realized immediately that our church was in a position to answer many of John's needs. The Lord touched my heart and immediately I realized that His hand had placed me at that meeting at that particular time.

John had to be accepted at a school which could provide the special education he was seeking. He needed financial support for his tuition, room, and board. He needed a "family" in a strange land.

Our area had one of the best schools in John's specialized field. One of our deacons was the Registrar of that university. He was quick to point out that the school had a high percentage of African students and also an excellent program to help the foreign students become a part of the American school. But neither the school nor the diocese could provide the necessary funds for John's education.

I called the National Church office to report on my progress at the school and discovered that financial support for John's education had been pouring into the Church headquarters. They would pay all his school fees, but they could not cover his room and board.

After a few minutes of thought, I put in a telephone call to the priest at one of our churches near the university, but while the phone was ringing he walked through the door of my office.

"I need," I told him outright, "free room and board for an African student in your community for as long as it takes him to complete four years of college." As I said that, I realized for the first time how much I was asking.

"You won't believe this," the priest replied (little realizing that by then I would believe anything), "but I have just been talking to a friend who is looking for a student to live with him. He lives alone in a large house and will provide room and board. The only payment he asks is some help keeping the house clean."

I knew that the man of whom he was speaking was an exceptionally fine Christian. When we called him, he was delighted at the prospect of having John come to live with him.

"All things work together for good to them that love God," says Romans 8:28. Right in our midst, a "marvelous thing" is being accomplished. John is realizing his dream of a college education which he will use to help his people.

What were the obstacles that could have prevented John from continuing his education?

_____

_____

_____

_____

What is the connection between worshiping God and the working of His miracles?

_____

_____

_____

_____

In the coming week, what can you do to increase your perception of God at work in the world?

_____

_____

_____

_____

Have you experienced, or known of, "coincidences" which revealed the "marvelous things" which God is doing in the world?

_____

_____

_____

_____

32

Spiritually Alert

The Christian disciple is not always "on the mountaintop" of joy and trust in God's marvelous presence. He comes down to face the reality of his own failure.

Overawed by our perceptions of what God is doing in the world, we "leave it all to Him" and fail to hear what He is asking us to do. We neglect the hard work of prayer.

Peter, James, and John went "to the mountaintop" and witnessed the transfiguration of our Lord. Read Matthew 17:14-21 and see what happened to them when they came down from the mountain.

Peter, James, and John moved from seclusion to public ministry and from mountaintop to plain. Jesus frequently withdrew from the crowds for periods of spiritual nourishment, but He always returned to use His spiritual power for teaching and healing the people.

From the glory of the mountaintop, Jesus and the three disciples returned to "the real world." It was a world of sickness, faithlessness, and approaching death. Jesus' apparent impatience is easy to understand when we consider the disciples' meager progress. After months of intensive teaching and training, their lack of faith had hindered their healing power.

In the shadow of my mountaintop experience with the African student, I had occasion to realize my own faithlessness and failure.

Our son, Crawford, a high school senior at the time, had worked summers and many weekends to save money for an eight-day trip to Europe. As the time for his trip approached, my wife and I became more and more anxious. The original plan for a trip with his own German class led by its teacher had disintegrated. Now, only Crawford and a sophomore girl we did not know would go to Kennedy Airport in New York, transfer to an airline we had never heard of, and fly off across the Atlantic with some students and teachers from Reno, Nevada.

As we drove to the airport on the morning of his departure, I tried desperately to think of all the things that Crawford should do or not do. I told him how to look after the sophomore, how to get the shuttle bus at Kennedy, and myriad details. I frantically offered up prayers that were not quite trusting, and I neglected to pray with Crawford for his journey. I failed to be spiritually attentive.

We arrived at the airport early and waited for the sophomore girl to show up. She didn't, and we grew more and more concerned at the idea of Crawford setting out alone. Even a sophomore was better than nothing!

In our panic, we failed completely in our Christian witness. We were spiritually impotent at a time when we should have been towers of strength for our son as he set out on his great adventure.

Later we learned that the sophomore had gotten on the plane and traveled with Crawford to New York. Our lack of faith, our failure to be alert spiritually, our worldly panic had kept us from seeing the girl.

What steps should Christian parents take to prepare a child spiritually for a "great adventure"?

_____

_____

_____

_____

List as many reasons as you can (besides the lack of faith) for the disciples' failure to heal.

_____

_____

_____

Where in your life are you spiritually impotent? How will you deal with this in the coming week?

_____

_____

_____

_____

Has there been an instance in your past when your failure to be spiritually alert resulted in spiritual impotence? What were your feelings?

_____

_____

_____

_____

33

Drawing Lines

Christian disciples are often guilty of drawing lines of resistance to tasks the Lord asks them to undertake. There is always something that is "going too far" or "expecting too much."

One cool summer evening I was sitting on a porch at a religious center chatting with several people who were experiencing new freedom in their faith. Sitting with us was an older clergyman who seemed to the rest of us to be a bit stuffy.

One by one, we related our experiences of prayer or worship, and each tried to demonstrate that he was "further out" than the person before him. At the end of each story, the old clergyman would grunt and say, "I can accept that."

The time came, however (as it was bound to come), when he groaned, "That's it! That's where I draw the line of rigidity."

Read Exodus 4:10-17.

Moses had drawn his lines of rigidity all over the place, giving one excuse after another for not doing what God was asking him to do. Finally, he used as an excuse his inability to speak effectively.

Perhaps one element of Moses' greatness was his determination to be honest with God, even if it meant arguing with his Creator. But his lack of eloquence was his weakest argument. "Who made your mouth?" God asked pointedly.

Moses used lack of ability as an excuse before the All-powerful who never fails to empower his children for the work He asks them to do. Moses' lack of trust in that power roused God's holy displeasure, yet He gave Aaron to Moses to be his mouthpiece and helper.

God won't let us off the hook; He always gives us the help we need to do His will.

Emma Lou Benignus tells a story which is a modern parallel to Moses and his excuses.[28] A Christian disciple, a young woman who worked as a research technician in a hospital, was asked a favor by a surgeon there.

A young man had been deprived by extensive surgery of the use of his legs and control of all the functions of his lower body. He wanted to die, and it was probable that he would. However, his deepest distress came not from facing death but from the loss of his manhood. The surgeon asked the technician to talk to the young man in more than a casual way and to relate to him as a woman to a man.

The technician agreed, but there was a condition which made it extremely difficult. The young man was also suffering from gangrenous peritonitis, and the resulting odor was foul. When the girl entered the patient's room for the first time, she was overwhelmed by the stench, gagged, and retreated down the hall.

Before she had gone far, however, she ran into the surgeon who firmly but kindly turned her around and led her back to the patient's room. "I know that it smells bad," he said, "but there is a man in there, a heartbroken young man. You are a woman. Go to him, and find the man inside that stink."

All that week the surgeon kept calling the girl to acts of selflessness as she ministered to the young man. He was reached and died in peace.

The technician was given the grace to cross over the line of rigidity which she had drawn, and another soul was brought closer to God. Later, as she meditated upon the Incarnation, she remembered the doctor's words and realized that God sent His Son into the world to find each one of us inside the human stink.

How could the technician reach the young man and help him cope with his problems?

_____

_____

_____

How do you suppose God felt as Moses kept drawing his lines of resistance to Him?

_____

_____

_____

_____

What line of resistance can you cross in the coming week?

_____

_____

_____

_____

Have you had an encounter with God when He asked you to do something you didn't want to do? Who won, and what happened?

_____

_____

_____

_____

34

Secularizing the Faith

Disciples of Christ must be wary of the ways of the world that seem harmless but which may have tragic results.

A friend of mine, a devoted Christian and a gifted artist, was asked by a large company to design a series of astrological symbols. She did, with some reservations, but later, when they asked her to design fortune-telling cards, she refused.

Many Christians study their horoscopes, wear astrological signs, and engage in secular fads which basically are contrary to the Christian faith. Even "slight deviations" from Christian standards can eventually lead to tragic consequences.

Read Deuteronomy 18:9-14.

In his newspaper column, evangelist Billy Graham commented once on this passage from Deuteronomy. In answer to a person who had asked under what sign of the zodiac Jesus was born, Dr. Graham pointed out that the Bible clearly condemns astrology.

The Jewish people, surrounded by pagan beliefs and practices, were cautioned repeatedly to avoid the secularization of their faith. They were specifically forbidden to engage in any form of divination.

Citing Isaiah 47:13 and Jeremiah 10:2, Dr. Graham noted that the prophets denounced astrology. Christians, too, know that it is God who is in control, and it is to Him that they should look for guidance.

Astrology denies that God is in control. Belief in the influence of the stars can lead to a belief in witchcraft, and from that an individual can fall under the influence of Satan.

God speaks to us through the Bible, through prayer, and through the church. We have no need of other devices. God reveals to us as much of the future as we need to know, and He guides us day by day. If people spent as much time reading the Bible as they do occupying themselves with worldly fads, their lives would be enriched immeasurably.

One day I went into a camera shop which I frequently patronize and found the salesgirl on duty unusually distressed. "I am a Virgo," she explained to me, "and things never go right for us."

"Surely, you don't believe all that stuff!" I replied immediately, and rather indelicately.

"Oh, I do," she answered, and proceeded to tell me that a friend who was an expert in such matters had assured her that she was destined for a series of personal disasters. Of course, in her distraught state it was quite possible that she would bring any number of unpleasant accidents upon herself.

I tried to reason with the girl but had little success. When I turned to leave, I found an Episcopal priest standing behind me listening to the girl's story. "I believe," he said to her, "that if I were you I'd change gods."

I was praying for the salesgirl when the Billy Graham article appeared in our local paper. I took it to the girl.

The next time I went into the shop, she was beaming. She took my hand and thanked me. "I've got it all straightened out now," she said.

"Baptizing" the ways of the world, the flesh, and the devil doesn't work, and can lead to unhappiness and even agony.

Christian disciples have God for their guide. They live under the sign of the Cross and have no need to "look to the stars."

What approach would you have used with the girl in the camera shop?

_____

_____

_____

_____

In the world today, what practices are related to those which are condemned in the Bible passage?

_____

_____

_____

_____

What will you say to the next person who asks you under which sign you were born (after you have said, "The Cross")?

_____

_____

_____

_____

Have you had a confrontation with anyone who believed in horoscopes or some related practice? What was the outcome? How did you feel?

_____

_____

_____

_____

35

The Joy of Giving

Generosity is an essential characteristic of Christian discipleship. But how can we respond to the multitude of needs in the world?

We should give first to the work of the Church in the world, and our standard should be the tithe (10%).

We must look at several Bible passages to see the complete picture of Christian giving.

1 Peter 4:10. Christians know that everything of value and of lasting benefit is a gift from God. How we use the gifts entrusted to our care is the measure of our stewardship.

1 Corinthians 4:1-2. Like any other steward, a Christian disciple should be faithful. But those things over which Christians have been given stewardship are greater than the things of the world. Disciples are called to a greater faithfulness. We shall have to account for all that we have and all that we are.

Luke 11:37-42. Tithing is an act of obedience. Long before Moses, God expected the Jews to tithe, and He expects it of us today. It is, for the people of God, the minimum offering to God. Down through the ages many Christians have given more than a tithe, and some have shared all that they possess with others.

1 Chronicles 29:10-17. David the king acknowledged God's goodness to His people. Everything had come from God, and all they offered back to Him was His also. "All that is in the heaven and in the earth is Thine." In this passage we see the joy of giving freely.

We are called to be faithful stewards of the gifts of God, to account to Him for what He has entrusted to us. Tithing is the base upon which we build our giving, and giving freely bears the fruit of joy.

Many well-intentioned Christians have never discovered the joy of giving. They give to the Church as a duty.

I was an agnostic for years until, in the early years of my marriage, I came to know the Lord. Even then, no one introduced me to Bible study or taught me about tithing. Yet, because of my relationship with the Lord, I wanted to make a serious commitment of my money (considerably less than a tithe, however) at the time of our church's stewardship canvass.

The canvasser who called on me was an older man and a prominent banker in our town. Although he had participated in the church's stewardship campaigns for years, he had seldom met a young man so eager to pledge. My enthusiasm caught him off guard.

"Now, don't get too generous," he cautioned. "After all, you are a young man with a wife and small children to provide for. The church will get by; don't worry about that. Just pledge what you know you can handle, and don't impose a financial burden on yourself."

My Christian convictions were not firmly set at that time, and it was easy for me to convince myself that my older and wiser friend was right. He was a fine person with my interests at heart. As a banker, he knew what I could and could not afford. So I reduced the amount of my pledge to the nominal amount of $7.00 a week.

The years passed, and as I studied the Bible and my faith grew stronger, I began to tithe. As I tithed, the Lord blessed me with abundance. It was not that my income increased; it was my values that changed. "Where my treasure was, my heart was also," and I moved into a closer relationship with the Lord.

I appreciated the banker's concern for me, but I realized that for several years I had been cheated of a great blessing.

I never miss an opportunity to encourage someone to tithe. Everyone can, and everyone should tithe. It is not important on what basis one tithes. Some give 5% to the Church and 5% to charity; some tithe before taxes and some after. If anyone asks me if he should tithe on his net or his gross income, I can say with conviction, "It depends on whether you want God to bless your net or your gross."

The Christian disciple does not tithe just to receive a blessing from the Lord, but he knows that willing obedience is in itself a blessing. It places his value system within God's will.

In your church's next stewardship campaign, if the canvasser advises you to be cautious, what will you answer?

_____

_____

_____

_____

Which of today's Bible passages has the most meaning for you?

_____

_____

_____

_____

Within the next week how will you determine if your stewardship program is in accord with God's will for you?

_____

_____

_____

_____

What has been your most memorable experience with generous giving?

_____

_____

_____

36

Receiving God's Forgiveness

Many Christians who have learned to forgive those who do them wrong have never been able to accept the Lord's forgiveness of their own sins. They carry their guilt about with them, adding one remembered sin to another until their Christian witness becomes a dull and joyless thing.

They have missed the heart of the Good News that "Christians aren't perfect, just forgiven." Our freedom lies in the fact that we can go to God, confess our sins to Him, and be completely absolved. God forgives our sins and forgets them; they are as far from His mind as the east is from the west.

God has always been willing to forgive those who truly repent. Read Psalm 32.

Psalm 32 was the favorite psalm of Augustine of Hippo, the great sinner who became a great saint. The psalm is a song of Thanksgiving, but its primary subject is penitence.

The psalmist begins with a burst of joy. A pure heart, he says, has no guile. Its sin is not concealed but confessed in openness and honesty before the Lord.

Verses 3-5 tell us of the psalmist's misery when he lived in sin, and he describes his condition in terms of physical illness. Pardon and healing come with the confession of his iniquity. When the godly have experienced forgiveness and learned its lessons, they will pass unharmed through days of trouble. The psalmist begs his listeners to heed his words, and the song ends with his invitation to share in the joy of forgiven sinners.

God forgives our grievous sins and sins which we have borne for years without repentance. And there is no freedom like that which comes when we know that He has forgiven us and will remember our sin no more.

The Christian disciple can be duped by Satan into believing that his sins have never been forgiven. Sins from his past, grievous sins and small nagging sins, will leap into his mind and weigh heavily on his heart.

Howard Ball tells of a farm boy who, as he went about his chores, was constantly bombarded with memories of sins which he had sincerely confessed years before.[29] He desperately sought relief from this burden with no result.

One day, through the grace of God, he found a solution to his problem. He realized that it was Satan who was reminding him of his sins. He stopped plowing and went behind the barn with an axe and a wooden stake. Once more he confessed to God all the sins which had been plaguing him. Then he carved the date on the wooden stake and drove it into the ground.

Later, when the sins came into his mind and he knew that Satan was trying to convict him once again, he stopped his work and went to the stake. "Do you see that stake, Satan?" he asked. "You can forget trying to remind me of that sin. I confessed it on April 12." After that, he had little trouble with his old sins.

But sometimes it is the Lord who recalls to our minds injuries we have inflicted upon others. We may have confessed the sins, but we have failed to take some action which He expects us to take. Perhaps we have not asked forgiveness from the person we injured. Perhaps we have failed to make restitution. But if we have confessed and done all we can to make things right again, we do not have to let the enemy haunt us with doubts.

Are there other ways the farm boy could have gotten Satan off his back?

_____

_____

_____

In addition to Psalm 32, find at least two other places in the Bible where God assures us that our sins are forgiven.

_____

_____

_____

During the coming week, what can you do to rid yourself of nagging guilt and find the assurance that your sins are forgiven?

_____

_____

_____

_____

How have you dealt effectively with unresolved guilt or unaccepted forgiveness?

_____

_____

_____

_____

37

A Great Commission

All Christian disciples are under the Great Commission to go forth into the world proclaiming Jesus Christ as Lord and Savior (Matt. 28:19-20).

Some Christians are called to be evangelists, while others find it difficult to lead people to accept the Lord. But not all of us are expected to be preachers and exhorters. What is more important is for us all to be able to speak naturally about our faith in Christ and pray with people whose hearts are ready to receive Him.

We are "seed sowers" and instruments which God can use in many ways to open people's eyes to the Light of Christ.

Read 1 Peter 3:15.

Originally, the epistle spoke to Christians living in a hostile and suspicious world. If we are honest, we must admit that we live in that kind of world today.

Each person must know the reason for the hope that is in him through Christ. It is important that we testify to our faith. We must tell what we were like before we met Christ, tell what He has done for us and what our life has been since He became our Lord and Savior. We must be able to explain who Christ is and what His death on the Cross meant to the world. That is our witness.

Too many Christians fail to examine, even for themselves, the reasons for their faith and what it really means to them. When they do determine these things, they are able to explain their faith to others intelligently and naturally. Peter did not tell us to win people to Christ by argument. Rather, he told Christians to avail themselves of opportunities to explain Christ to others.

Our statement of belief, Peter said, should not be belligerent as those whose vociferous arguments betray their own doubts. The unbeliever can sniff out a phony Christian as expertly as a bloodhound. Our attitude must be one of "meekness and fear," which is gentleness and reverence.

God uses people in many different ways to bring other people to Christ.

Mabel had known Tom and his family for many years, first as neighbors and later as friends. Then Tom, who was a salesman, moved his family to a city about fifty miles away.

Mabel, an older widow, kept up with Tom and his family when the young man's business brought him back periodically to their hometown.

Tragedy struck Tom when his wife divorced him and won custody of their children. Working as a traveling salesman was all that Tom had ever done, and his life became increasingly miserable. When his work took him to the city where his children were living, his wife always had reasons for keeping them from him.

The situation was tearing Tom apart, and as hard as Mabel tried, she was not able to help him.

But one night in a motel room, Tom in desperation picked up a Gideon Bible and found the Lord.

Mabel was overjoyed to hear of Tom's newly discovered faith, but she soon became concerned about two things. First, she herself had trouble communicating to Tom what her faith meant to her. She was from a traditional church and talked about her faith in "Old English." Tom's knowledge of the faith came from his Bible reading amplified by his own interpretations.

Mabel was distressed, too, that Tom would have nothing to do with the church. He had found God in a motel room through the Bible, and he saw no need to become part of the Christian fellowship. What is more, Tom's avid but unenlightened study of the Bible was leading him to strange conclusions.

Mabel knew that Tom must join a church, but she knew that she alone could not bring it about. So she prayed for him. She asked many others to pray for him. She talked to as many people as she could, asking for their advice on how to tell Tom of her hopes for him. She found people for Tom to talk with and books for him to read. She kept praying. The day finally came when she was able to write to tell me that Tom had been baptized in her church on Easter Eve.

"The events that led to this turnabout have been nothing short of miraculous. Tom is so happy that he is about to pop!"

Mabel was faithful; she had persevered. She was Christ's witness in every way she could be, and her witness bore abundant fruit.

What advice would you have given Mabel if she had asked you how she could communicate with Tom?

_____

_____

_____

_____

What is the reason for the hope that is in you?

_____

_____

_____

_____

To whom does God ask you to witness? What will you do about it in the coming week?

_____

_____

_____

_____

What is your most interesting experience in leading, or attempting to lead, others to Christ?

_____

_____

_____

_____

38

Christian Maturity

As we have studied Christian discipleship together, we hope that we have moved toward a more mature relationship with God. Too often we judge one person to be more "spiritual" than another when what we really see is a person who is more spiritually mature.

As in every process of maturing, growth occurs as a result of time and the effect of the experiences encountered during that time. An apple matures because of the length of time it is on the tree and the effects of weather during that time. Although a space of time is essential, the effects of experience are perhaps vastly more important to the maturing process.

This is particularly true with individuals. A baby cannot be mature physically or mentally; he hasn't been around long enough. But many young people are much more mature than their elders because of what they have learned from the experiences they have had.

Read James 1:1-8.

The Christian disciple accepts standards which are much higher than those of the world about him, and he is bound to face trials and temptations. However, the trials can be occasions for rejoicing (Matt. 5:11-12).

There is joy in Christian endurance, for in suffering patiently we share the joy of Christ who "for the joy that lay ahead of Him, endured the cross" (Heb. 12:2). The faith and endurance with which we meet and overcome our trials mature us. Real and complete maturity, of course, was achieved only once on earth—by Christ Himself, the completed man.

James lists the qualities which lead to maturity. *Patience* comes from testing our faith. If we lack *wisdom,* we should *pray* for it. We must be *single-minded*—no half-heartedness or half-measures for the Christian disciple.

Joe Bishop learned a lot about maturity with the sudden death of his teen-aged son and the lingering death of his wife. When he wrote of these events, he began by recounting an experience he had had years before.[30]

Bishop and his family were at their summer home in Rhode Island when a hurricane struck the eastern seaboard. Furious winds lifted houses and flung them down half a mile inland. From their living room window, the Bishops watched the sea pound through a sand bar which separated their salt-water pond from the ocean itself. They watched the pond waters rise rapidly up the hill on which their house was perched.

Because the power lines were down, Joe Bishop fought his way to his car to listen to the weather report on the car radio. The worst of the storm was upon them, he heard, and if they were on high ground they were to stay where they were.

As Bishop headed back to his house, the roaring wind suddenly stopped. All around him the storm raged, but where he stood was "immense calm." He was in the eye of the storm.

Later, Joe Bishop read an article entitled, "The Way Out Is the Way Through." One must meet the trials of life head-on, it said, and work through them to the other side. God's power is available at the point of faith, and His grace will show us the way. It is when we turn aside and flee from the storm that we are defeated, for we do not allow God to help us through.

Joe Bishop found that the answers to the problems of life are in the center of the problems themselves. "The peace of the Lord is discovered in the eye of the storm."

Christian maturity comes to us as we face the problems of life head-on and, with God's help, work through them.

Does "the eye of the storm" resemble "the peace that passeth understanding"?

_____

_____

_____

Are there other characteristics of Christian maturity than those mentioned by James in the Bible passage?

_____

_____

_____

_____

What problem have you been avoiding which you will meet head-on during the coming week?

_____

_____

_____

_____

Have you had a problem which you met head-on when it would have been easier to side step? What did you experience as you worked through the problem?

_____

_____

_____

_____

39

Reactions

The way we react is a test of our maturity as Christian disciples. For good reasons or bad, Christians and non-Christians alike can control their actions. It is more difficult to control their reactions.

To control our actions, all we must do is decide to act in a certain way, or to refrain from acting in that way. To control our reaction, our immediate response to what someone does to us, is not as easy, if it is possible at all.

The only way we can control our reactions is to locate within ourselves the problem which brings forth a bad response. By God's grace we may overcome the problem and change our negative reactions to good ones.

Read Acts 6:8-15.

Stephen was a classic example of a man who reacted in a godly manner. He was filled with grace and power. Grace is both God's favor and a virtuous personality. Power was evident in Stephen. Through him, the early Church had become a threat to Judaism's religion and life. What had appeared to be merely a sect was gaining more and more followers, some of whom were Jewish priests.

God's Holy Spirit worked mightily in Stephen. He was so effective in debate and revolutionary in his arguments that he was brought to trial on two counts: blaspheming against God for prophesying the overthrow of the Temple; and rebellion against Moses for contending that the Law had been replaced by Christ.

Young Stephen was brought before the High Council of the land, convicted by false witnesses, and condemned to death by those who had been stirred up maliciously against him. And what was Stephen's reaction? His face was as "the face of an angel."

Stephen argued in his own defense, but he did so in order to teach; he showed no animosity. He was condemned to death by stoning, but he asked God to forgive his executioners and commended himself into the Lord's hands.

The grace and power integral to Stephen's very being produced positive reactions for him. His strength was in the Lord.

So many of my reactions have been different from Stephen's! During my pre-Christian years, I was fairly popular by worldly standards. I had many friends and was elected to various offices and positions of prominence.

My popularity was important to me. As I reflect on that period of my life, I realize that my popularity was essential for me. I continually looked for reassurance that I was well-liked. Like a chameleon adapting its colors to its surroundings, I accommodated myself to the crowd I was with at any particular time. I needed acceptance. Nothing discouraged me so much as an unkind remark or a defeat, and I could not tolerate criticism.

As the years passed, the Lord blessed me with insight into my reactions. I came to see that my inability to cope with criticism came from my devotion to myself, the epitome of self-centeredness. As Christ became the center of my life, criticism of myself did not trouble me so much.

Coping with unpleasant letters had always been more difficult for me than coping with unpleasant remarks. (Remarks can always be blamed on a fit of temper, but written remarks imply conviction.) But now, instead of composing angry replies to such letters, I can see them as opportunities for showing Christ's love. I can see that the writer had a genuine concern which prompted him to write, and I try to look at the matter from his point of view. I submit the letter and my reply to the Lord in prayer.

The results have amazed me. As I have written replies, I have been given insights and inspiration. I have had a sense of being the Lord's instrument to reach and touch a person He wants me to love. People who could have become my enemies are now my friends.

In all our daily confrontations God wishes us to react with love. If we can reflect on our bad reactions and consider the problems within ourselves which bring them forth, God will give us grace to turn potentially unpleasant encounters into opportunities for love.

How did you respond to the last nasty letter you received?

_____

_____

_____

_____

How do you think Stephen felt as he was brought to trial? How would you have felt?

_____

_____

_____

_____

What bad reaction of your own will you try to get to the bottom of in the coming week?

_____

_____

_____

_____

Think of a confrontation in your past. Could you have, or did you, react with love? What happened, and what were the results?

_____

_____

_____

40

A Philosophy of Death

A look at death and eternal life concludes our study of Christian discipleship. What to most non-Christians is the ultimate disaster is for Christian disciples the doorway to a glorious future. Death, however traumatic it may be physically, is a continuation of "The Way," the joys about which we have received only hints. Death is graduation from the School of Life.

A disciple must have a philosophy of death. Too many Christians have a mistaken idea of death because they have never fully understood life in Christ. They focus on the good things which will be their reward for the bad things they have borne on earth. Paul did not share this point of view. He saw a larger picture.

Read Philippians 1:19-30.

The letter to the Philippians is a letter of joy. The words "joy" and "rejoice" appear sixteen times in the Epistle, yet it was written in suffering. Joy then has a greater meaning than "happiness." Here we talk of the joy of abiding in Christ.

To Paul, neither life nor death was the issue. If he died, he would have the joy of the greater presence of Christ. If he lived, he would be of further service to those Christ had given to him. He wanted only to stand firm in Christ and be of service regardless of the consequences.

Paul encouraged the Philippians, too, to stand firm. "Let your conduct be worthy of the Gospel of Christ," as the New English Bible translates it. The Philippians were exhorted to be one in spirit, one in mind against their opponents. They had the privilege not only of believing in Christ but also, with Paul, of suffering for Him.

Suffering bound the Philippians to Paul, but, more important, it bound them to Christ Himself. Thus, it was a privilege to endure, and suffering became the guarantee of belonging to Christ. "To live is Christ, and to die is gain."

Paul was not the only disciple with a right understanding of death. Emily Gardiner Neal tells about a woman in the terminal stages of cancer.[31]

The woman had flown to a healing service conducted by Miss Neal at Calvary Church in Pittsburgh, where Miss Neal met with her for a short time before the service. When the woman came into the room the Light of Christ shone forth from her very being.

Miss Neal asked her if she were afraid to die. "Oh, no," the woman answered. "Actually, I long to be wholly with Christ. But life is a gift from God, and I feel I must do everything possible to preserve it, for there may be more He wants me to do here. That is why I have come to Pittsburgh to attend this healing service."

That woman had the answer, the Christian answer, to life and death. Regardless of the state of her body, whether she lived or died, she was whole.

Miss Neal's years of counseling and praying with the sick and dying have convinced her that we cannot live a full Christian life without having a Christian philosophy of death. We cannot know the abundant life our Lord came to give us unless we are unafraid of death, unless we know every moment that we are living in the midst of eternal life.

What is your philosophy of death?

_____

_____

_____

_____

What is Paul's philosophy of death? Does it differ from yours?

_____

_____

_____

_____

How can you minister to a fellow Christian who is dying?

_____

_____

_____

_____

Have you helped a person cope with death—or seen another person helping? What did you learn from that experience which will help you later?

_____

_____

_____

_____

Footnotes

[1]Robert L. Howell, *Fish for My People* (New York: Morehouse-Barlow Co., 1968), pp. 89-90.

[2]Father Andrew, *The Pattern Prayer* (London: A. R. Mowbray & Co., Ltd., 1942), p. 77.

[3]Larry Christenson, *The Christian Family* (Minneapolis: Bethany Fellowship, Inc., 1970), p. 209.

[4](Grand Rapids: Wm. B. Eerdmans Publishing Co., 1970), p. 1103.

[5]Keith Miller, *A Second Touch* (Waco, Texas: Word Books, 1967), p. 58.

[6]C. S. Lewis, *Mere Christianity* (New York: Macmillan Publishing Co., Inc., 1960), pp. 55-56.

[7]Clyde S. Kilby, editor, *A Mind Awake, An Anthology of C. S. Lewis* (New York: Harcourt, Brace and World, Inc., 1968), pp. 122-123.

[8]Christenson, p. 175.

[9]Father Andrew, *Christ the Companion* (London: A. R. Mowbray & Co., Ltd., 1959), p. 110.

[10]Father Andrew, *The Seven Signs of Christ* (London: A. R. Mowbray & Co., Ltd., 1944), pp. 60-61.

[11]Rosalind Rinker, *You Can Witness with Confidence* (Grand Rapids: Zondervan Publishing House, 1962), pp. 25-26.

[12]Ernest Gordon, *Through the Valley of the Kwai* (New York: Harper & Row, 1962).

[13]Miller, pp. 63-64.

[14]Cecil B. Murphey, *Prayer Pitfalls and Possibilities* (New York: Hawthorn Books, Inc., 1975), pp. 36-37.

[15]Father Andrew, *The Pattern Prayer*, pp. 36-37.

[16]John and Karen Howe, *Which Way?* (New York: Morehouse-Barlow Co., 1973), p. 90.

[17]Christenson, pp. 189-190.

[18]Stephen Verney, *Fire in Coventry* (London: Hodder and Stoughton, 1964), p. 32.

[19]Charles W. Colson, *Born Again* (Old Tappan, New Jersey: Fleming H. Revell Company, 1977).

[20]Helen S. Shoemaker, *Prayer Is Action* (New York: Morehouse-Barlow Co., 1969), pp. 30-31.

[21]William Barclay, *The Daily Study Bible* (Philadelphia: The Westminster Press, 1954), "The Letters to the Corinthians," p. 61.

[22]John A. Sanford, *The Kingdom Within* (Philadelphia and New York: J. B. Lippincott Company, 1970), pp. 15-17.

[23]Murphey, pp. 96-97.

[24]Emily Gardiner Neal, *The Healing Power of Christ* (New York: Hawthorn Books, Inc., 1972), pp. xi-xii.

[25]Verney, p. 32.

[26]Barclay, "The Gospel of John, Volume 2," p. 92.

[27]Charles F. Whiston, *Teach Us to Pray* (Boston: The Pilgrim Press, 1949), pp. 155-156.

[28]Taken from the "Action Information" newsletter of The Alban Institute, Mount St. Alban, Washington, D.C. 20016.

[29]Taken from a story told by Howard Ball, president of Churches Alive!, Box 3800, San Bernardino, CA 92413.

[30]Joseph P. Bishop, *The Eye of the Storm* (Lincoln, Virginia: Chosen Books, 1976), pp. 7-8.

[31]Neal, pp. 12-13.